Mot[illegible]

in[illegible]

Motor Racing in Colour

DOUG NYE

BLANDFORD PRESS
POOLE DORSET

First published 1978

Link House, West Street,
Poole, Dorset, BH15 1LL

ISBN 0 7137 0904 9

Printed in Great Britain by
Richard Clay (The Chaucer Press) Ltd
Bungay, Suffolk
Colour plates printed by
Sackville Press Billericay Ltd

Contents

Introduction

Today, motor racing at all its many levels is one of the most popular spectator sports in the world. More than a million people flock to watch the World Championship races of each year, fought out by highly sophisticated Formula 1 cars and the most talented drivers of their day on circuits from Buenos Aires in Argentina, through Long Beach on America's West Coast, across to Europe and the classical venues such as Monte Carlo, then back to North America in the autumn.

Yet while Grand Prix racing is the much-publicised showcase of modern motor sport, there is far more activity – worldwide – lower down the scale. Sports cars, grand touring cars, production saloon cars, a bewildering array of 'proper' single-seater racing car classes, all abound. They are raced in all parts of the world, from up near the Arctic Circle in Finland and way down towards the southern Pole at Invercargill in the South Island of New Zealand.

Motor racing is at its most intense in Europe, with club level race meetings at their most prolific in Great Britain, where barely a weekend goes by without a half-dozen fixtures on permanent circuits throughout the country. In the USA, road racing is still a rather staid and genteel poor relation to some highly-specialised brands of oval track competition. All kinds of motor sport flourish on a national if not international level throughout the more prosperous countries of South America. Across the Atlantic, motor racing has a firm foothold in South Africa; it is established across the Pacific in Japan and other countries of the Far East, and it seems certain that oil-rich enthusiasts in the Middle East will be fostering serious motor sport out there in the desert dust.

Motor racing is unusual in that at top level its strong sporting element has always been inextricably linked with technological development and advance, and with commercial and industrial publicity and promotion. It has been with us virtually since the earliest dawn of motoring itself. In fact, as early as 1878, eight years before Carl Benz and Gottlieb Daimler persuaded their petrol-engined horseless carriages to clatter into life, an 'automobile' race was promoted from Green Bay to Madison, Wisconsin, USA. It drew entries for six steamers, of which two started and one finished – the winning Oshkosh having averaged around 6 mph in an 18-day event, including tests for load-hauling and ploughing ability! The unfortunate Cowles 'Green Bay' steamer had a troubled time before expiring finally only 20 miles from the finish of the 201-mile course.

As early as 1887, just two years after Benz had produced what is generally accepted to have been the first practical gasoline-engined motor carriage, the first race was being organised in France. It was a false and unsuccessful sprint, and enthusiasts had to wait another seven years before the famous Paris–Rouen 'Rally' of 1894 introduced competitive motoring with a multiple entry.

One year later, in 1895, motor racing began in earnest. In Italy on the 29th May five widely divergent vehicles staggered off on a 62-mile race from Turin to the village of Asti and back again. Twelve days later, the infinitely more significant race from Paris to Bordeaux and back was flagged away, over an incredible course of no less than 745 miles! There were 22 starters from an entry of 97. Emile Levassor drove his Daimler Phénix-engined 3½-hp Panhard single-handed for 48 hr 48 min, virtually non-stop, to come home first after averaging 15·07 mph.

That was little more than eighty years ago. Less than a conceivable human lifespan. In that period, our technological learning curve has soared at an accelerating rate. The first man has flown in a heavier-than-air machine – and man has set foot on the moon, with millions watching 'live' television images of him doing so. Motor racing and the other 'gasoline sports' have blossomed concurrently, and at their highest levels as with other less sophisticated sporting activities they have become international big business. Motor racing development suffered badly from the interruption caused by two world wars; has reflected times of economic strength and weakness; and has been banned completely

The incredible Emile Levassor's Panhard 'No 5' leaves Versailles at the start of the Paris–Bordeaux–Paris race in 1895, which he led home after an heroic 48-hour single-handed drive. There was no concession to streamlining in these early cars, and little weather protection.

by one nation and actively supported and even wielded as a political weapon by others.

Motor racing's face has changed quite dramatically in recent years, and although many enthusiasts are steadfastly convinced that it is better today than it has ever been, others bewail the passing of the days of linen helmets and of circuits fringed by trees and lamp-posts.

In this book we will look at the birth and development of motor racing at all its levels. We will look at how it all began, how it evolved and grew, how different branches sprouted and how they have flourished, or have withered and died.

But this has to be more than merely a story of what has happened in historic motor races. The design and construction of racing cars as a pinnacle of automotive efficiency is a still-developing science. Driving the designers' products to the ultimate limits of their efficiency, and often venturing beyond those bounds, is a still-developing art.

So we shall examine the technology required in motor racing today – and in the past – and trace the development of Grand Prix racing to the incredibly competitive peak we see today, when 26 cars on a Grand Prix grid can be separated by less than one second in lap times. The merest blink of an eye can reflect the difference between World Champion and also-ran; yet to wring that last ounce of speed from car and driver can easily break man, machine and business – and in many cases it has.

Naturally, the story of these men would not be complete without some appraisal of what they do, and of how they do it. Driving a racing car is not as simple as the popular image of a jut-chinned hero, crushing the accelerator pedal to the floor and bulleting fearlessly away around a circuit, might have us believe.

Professional race driving is an athletic pursuit. It demands incredible sensitivity, perception, balance, physical and psychological strength, concentration and determination, all combined with that barely definable 'killer instinct' – that overwhelming will to win.

So we shall discuss in the following pages the ingredients which make motor racing, at all levels, the most demanding of modern sports, a game played for keeps where mistakes, misjudgements and sheer misfortune may always cost not merely time nor points, but life itself. This is the colourful story of one of the most demanding sports – the story of motor racing.

1 From the Start

The first major motor race was run in 1895 over a staggeringly ambitious course – from the French capital city of Paris to the Atlantic port of Bordeaux and back. Today, such an event, covering 732 miles of public roads, would be utterly impossible to stage as a race. It could be run only as a rally.

A modern Grand Prix race (which is admittedly run for far more specialised vehicles than Levassor's spindly winning Panhard in 1894) covers a distance of no more than 200 miles and often occupies less time than a soccer match. The night and day difference is that whereas Levassor's 3½-hp Panhard averaged 15 mph during his two-day drive, and may perhaps have reached 30 mph flat-out, modern Grand Prix cars have 480 hp-plus and can average 130 mph or more during races on circuits where their maximum speed may be over 180 mph.

France was the seat of motor racing from those earliest days. In 1887, a Monsieur Fossier, editor of the magazine *La Vélocipede*, organised his first sprint race for 'automobiles' along the bank of the River Seine from St James to Neuilly. Only one vehicle started, Albert de Dion's steam-engined De Dion quadricycle, and it enjoyed a walk-over victory. In 1888, Fossier ran a second race, this time from Neuilly to Versailles, and a De Dion won again, this time from a Serpollet steamer.

The lack of visible competition in these embryo events effectively killed them, and it was not until the 1890s that petrol-engined vehicles began to appear and interest was renewed in horseless carriage competition.

The incentive was provided by public ignorance of automobile potential. It was left to another journalist, Pierre Giffard of the magazine *Le Petit Journal*, to organise a competition which would demonstrate to all just what the new invention could achieve. In the 19th December issue of 1893, *Le Petit Journal* announced a trial to be conducted from Paris to Rouen, along the Seine valley. The winner was to be decided by a judging panel, on the basis of the vehicle being '. . . without danger, easily handled and of low running cost'. The course was 31 miles and the entry had to complete it within 3 hours. Subsequently, this 10 mph average speed was considered too dangerous, and the time limit was extended by an hour.

There were 102 entries, many thoroughly optimistic as they listed motive power sources as varied as steam, petrol, compressed air, electricity, pedals, 'a system of levers', pendula and even gravity!

Predictably various problems, including the unreadiness of a large part of the entry, caused the Paris–Rouen Trial to be postponed, but on 22nd July 1894, 21 starters left the Boulevard

The Count de Dion and his hybrid motor wagon which was first home in the pioneering Paris–Rouen Trial of 1894, but which was ruled out because the adapted horse carriage trailer was not truly 'automobile'.

Maillot startline at 30-second intervals. Count de Dion's steam tractor, towing a conventional horse carriage minus front axle, was first to arrive in Rouen's Champ de Mars, having averaged 11·6 mph. The judges, however, refused to recognise this device as a true 'automobile' and the 5,000 Franc (£200) first prize was awarded jointly to the Peugeot brothers and to Emile Levassor. Both drove vehicles powered by Gottlieb Daimler's German patent petrol engines.

This Paris–Rouen Trial was more significant than its form might suggest, since it drew together all of France's motoring pioneers. Before the year ended a group of them had formed the *Automobile Club de France* – the ACF – and they began to plan the incredible test of both man and machine which was the Paris–Bordeaux–Paris race, and which made Emile Levassor and his Panhard car nationally famous.

This was an important result of motor racing, for other manufacturers were quick to note the fulsome publicity attracted by the Panhard performance. The race itself set a fashion for point-to-point cross-country races which was to survive (just) into the twentieth century.

In turn, the spread of cross-country, or city-to-city racing, fostered improvements in main route surfacing and maintenance and so generally accelerated the development of high-speed road travel – in competition with the established pace of the railways.

Early on, as in the 1890s, roads were still poor with innumerable potholes, savage drain gulleys and ruts. Weather equipment such as hoods and sidescreens were virtually unknown on the cars themselves and many of the countryside peasants remained convinced that the appearance of a horseless carriage was a visitation from the Devil himself.

The great race of 1896 was over no less than 1,062 miles, from Paris to Marseilles on the Mediterranean coast and back. It was run through savage storms and fell to Mayade's Panhard at an average of 15·7 mph. Tragically, Levassor's sister car crashed when he swerved to avoid a stray dog, and the great businessman–driver suffered a severe head injury, the after-effects of which probably caused his sudden death the following year.

Across the Atlantic, the first American motoring competition had been a desperately dull affair, organised by the *Chicago Times-Herald* in November 1895. Snow, and public-befuddling regulations, ruined the event and in 1896 the New York *Cosmopolitan* magazine race did further damage to the embryo sport.

A contemporary report of the *Cosmopolitan* event read:

> *'Six horseless carriages, entered for a drive, Wheel came off one, then there were five; Five horseless carriages, racing as before, Chain slipped on one, and then there were four, Four horseless carriages, speeding merrily, Bicycle ran into one, and then there were three; Three horseless carriages, came to a hill, Hill stayed right where it was, so the drivers had to get off and push, and that was why the time between City Hall and Irvington for the prize of 3,000 dollars offered by a magazine was not what it might have been had there not been any hill there!'*

The same year saw the first track race run over five laps of a one-mile dirt course at Narragansett Park, Cranston, Rhode Island, where A. H. Whiting's Riker electric car beat seven competitors to average a blinding 24 mph. This form of racing, on an enclosed track where the crowd could be properly controlled, where free entry was virtually an impossibility (making race promotion profitable for the promoter) and where the spectators could see the whole course clearly, was to swamp road racing in the USA.

European tastes were on a more grand scale, and the great city-to-city races engulfed Europe. Organisers enforced overnight rest halts, there were passage controls on either side of townships along the route, and speed limits and driving restrictions were rigidly enforced through the towns themselves. These moves protected both competitor and spectator, but just picture the scene as the high-built and fragile vehicles of the 1890s tore around Europe with their crews exposed to the worst the weather could offer, and in some cases carrying passengers who went along just 'for the thrill of speed . . .'

Inter-marque rivalry was extreme, and even in these earliest days motor racing success was regarded as a passport to general sales success. Racing versions of the manufacturers' production cars were quickly developed, and within months the city-to-city racers from Panhard, Peugeot and De Dion bore little more than passing resemblance to the cars one could buy.

Already there was a lesser division of racing, in which the wealthy enthusiasts of the time entered and drove their production models in various events.

The result of such rivalry and intensive sales promotion was an accelerated rate of development. The speeds of racing spiralled, and by 1899 the fastest cars were reaching 50–60 mph – with minimal directional stability and derisory brakes.

The nine years of city-to-city racing from 1895 to 1903 were dominated initially by Panhard. In 1898 the *Course de Périgueux* was run over one lap of a circuit of public roads to provide a glimpse of what was to come in place of point-to-point or out-and-back racing. Sadly this event also saw the first immediately fatal racing accident, when the Marquis de Montaignac and his mechanic died after their Landry et Beyroux capsized. This vehicle, like Levassor's early Panhard, had been tiller-steered and the incident speeded the widespread adoption of wheel-steering which contributed greatly to increased performance and better car control.

Paris was the centre of the motor racing world, and races radiated from the French capital year after year. At the turn of the century, Mors cars began to topple Panhard from their pinnacle as the greatest road racers in Europe, while smaller and more scientifically designed cars from Renault and Mercedes (*née* Daimler) began to make their names.

Inter-marque rivalry was all-important, but national industries (like the French, which was the biggest) would join forces against any common enemy. A newspaper proprietor named James Gordon Bennett perceived this trait, and in 1899 his Parisian edition of the *New York Herald* was selected as stake-holder for a 'which car is best' wager between Fernand Charron – the French racing driver – and American manufacturer Alexander Winton.

Bennett had an eye for a good promotion, and he promptly put up a Challenge Cup for an international race series to be contested by teams of no more than three cars each chosen to represent their home country's industry. The ACF was to organise the maiden competition in 1900 with a race from Paris to Lyons, and the Trophy was then to be held by the winning country's national sporting authority, who were to organise the following year's event on their home soil.

Unfortunately, the Gordon Bennett series held the seeds of its own destruction within these regulations, as the provision of a single three-car team for each country was made regardless of each nation's individual motor industry strength. In fact, only the French had sufficient competition-orientated marques to pursue an active policy of team selection, and their manufacturers came to resent the equality with the British, Germans and Americans which Bennett's rules suggested. This resentment came to a head when they were beaten!

Deep rifts were caused within the ACF itself when their team choice for the inaugural Gordon Bennett race of 1900 was challenged. The race was to be run from Paris–Lyon, but in the preceding Paris–Roubaix event a crashing car had injured the wife of a French Parliamentary Deputy. Every race competitor was arrested on criminal charges and the future of motor racing in France was in jeopardy until influential members of the ACF managed to have the Gordon Bennett race reprieved at the last moment.

The French team included three Panhards, but all they faced was a solitary Belgian Bolide and an American Winton. Two of the Panhards were the only finishers in this farcical race, and Charron won from Girardot, averaging 38·6 mph for the 353-mile distance.

This 'success' gave the ACF the right to organise the second Gordon Bennett race in 1901, and they merely incorporated it as a class within the Paris–Bordeaux of that year. Another fiasco saw Girardot's Panhard the only official team member to finish – and he was tenth in the race overall. If the French could have won the Trophy for the third time in 1902, it would have been theirs in perpetuity and they could forget the competition – as indeed had its creator. Instead, the smug French industry had its team cars fail in the Paris–Innsbruck section of a major event racing on to Vienna, and the Trophy came to England thanks to S. F. Edge's Napier – which was the sole-surviving Bennett team entry.

Having been rescued by the British, the Trophy was next contested over a road course at Ballyshannon in Ireland in 1903, and there Camille Jenatzy won it for Mercedes and Germany. In 1904 the German authority ran the event over a similar closed-circuit public road course in the Taunus Hills and there Léon Théry won the Trophy for Richard-Brasier and France. The ACF selected a tortuous course in the Auvergne for the 1905 Gordon Bennett race, and Théry retained the trophy.

By this time, the French industry had decided that the restrictive three-car entry of the Gordon Bennett series was totally unacceptable, and they had laid plans to run their own 'Grand Prix' race – open to more numerous entries from various nations in proportion to the strength of their industries – during 1905. Other countries were enraged, notably Great Britain, but although the ACF backed down for 1905 they then allowed the Bennett series to lapse and ran the Grand Prix alone in 1906. This was the start of the premier form of international motor sport, which has survived to this day.

Meanwhile, circuit racing itself had replaced the heroic age of city-to-city racing. In 1900, the *Course du Catalogue* had been run over two laps of a triangular 45-mile closed public road circuit near Melun in northern France. This was the first time that a major field had passed the same way, in the same direction, more than once in a single event. The winner was Leonce Girardot, and the modern concept of reconnaissance and practice laps had become feasible.

One week later, the more important circuit race of the *Course du Sud-Ouest* was held outside Pau in southern France, and it was won by the ACF's founder member and leading official, the *Chevalier* Rene de Knyff. Still, closed-circuit racing was not to achieve major stature until 31st July 1902 when the *Circuit des Ardennes* (over six laps of a 53-mile circuit near Bastogne in Belgium) was won by Britain's Charles Jarrot – in the inevitable

Panhard – at an heroic average of 54 mph for the 318 miles.

Racing was firmly established in France, Italy, Belgium and Germany by this time, but despite French pre-eminence there had been a flutter in 1901 when parliamentary questions were asked about racing safety and a temporary ban had been imposed. The aristocratic committee of the ACF still wielded considerable influence, however, and since they insisted they wished merely to organise one major event each year the ban was eased.

City-to-city racing continued into 1903, when the ACF decided its major event would be a charge from Paris to the Spanish capital of Madrid. Prospects looked bleak as first the Pau races and then the Nice–Salon–Nice race were both refused permits by the French authorities and a licence for Paris–Madrid was withheld; but then King Alfonso of Spain granted the ACF a licence to run the race section from the border post at Irun to Madrid, and French opposition crumbled.

The race began on 24th May 1903 and a trail of disaster, mayhem and death marked its progress to Bordeaux where the authorities stopped it, impounded all competing vehicles, and shipped them back to Paris by rail. The specialised racing cars of the day were demonstrably too fast for the narrow roads and huge and uncontrolled crowds which flooded them. Louis Renault started third from Versailles and 20 miles from the start, just after Rambouillet, he was in the lead. On the straight tree-lined section between Bonneval and Chateaudun his light car *averaged* 90 mph!

In his wake gruesome accidents occurred and at Couhé-Verac – a small town between Poitiers and Ruffec – his brother Marcel's car overturned and fatally injured its crew. Out in front, Louis Renault thundered into Bordeaux 5 hr 29 min after leaving the Parisian startline at Versailles, having averaged 62·3 mph ... something it is difficult to do today, even with modern *autoroutes* to follow.

But Renault was not to win this stage, for in his wake was the fearless Fernand Gabriel, whose sharp-nosed 70-hp Mors had drawn 168th place at the start and had torn through clouds of choking dust and exhaust fumes, accidents and crash debris to finish third on the road at Bordeaux – and to beat Louis Renault into second place with an average speed of 65·3 mph! The accidents claimed two drivers, three mechanics and at least one of an estimated three-million spectators. It was the end of the city-to-city era.

While circuits consisting of closed public road loops became the norm as a motor racing venue, so technical developments began to produce the basic recipe for the sport we know today.

At the turn of the century racing cars in general had covered a wide range of sizes, from such monsters as a 10-litre Mors to the tiniest *voiturettes* (literally 'carlets') of just a few hundred cubic centimetres swept volume. The Renault brothers, whose successful partnership had been broken so cruelly by the Couhé–Verac tragedy, had been prominent among the voiturette and light car classes.

Marcel Renault, winner of the 1902 Paris–Vienna and his mechanic in their Renault 16hp 4-cylinder Light Car at the weigh-in, Place de la Concorde, Paris, on June 24, 1902. The driver was killed in the tragic Paris–Madrid the following year.

By 1901, the ACF had formalised four car classes, based on weight, since large engines were necessarily heavy at that time. The classes were for cyclecars, below 250 kg; for voiturettes, below 400 kg; for light cars, from 400–650 kg; and for heavy cars, over 650 kg. In practice, the voiturettes and light cars became virtually synonymous, and the Renault brothers' products were typical in this division, having grown from single-cylinder 499-cc 'thumpers' in 1900, through a 3·7-litre which carried Marcel to victory in the 1902 Paris–Vienna, to a 6·3-litre (lighter than 650 kg) for Paris–Madrid. In that event, these cars faced 12-litre models from Mors, 12½-litres from Mercedes and 13½-litres from Panhard – and their searing pace and evident controllability (in relative terms) stunned the established heavy car manufacturers. They, however, had considerable influence within the sporting authorities and as the lightweight construction of these very fast light cars was regarded with distaste following the Paris–Madrid disasters, so only the *Circuit des Ardennes* offered a small car class in 1904–5.

At this time more political problems appeared in France as Prime Minister Combes promised that road racing in that country was finished, once and for all. Still, the fireproof ACF won a special dispensation, and were allowed to run the 1904 Gordon Bennett Eliminating Trial (to choose their team) on a 58·2-mile circuit in the sparsely populated Argonne region.

While the French and other continental nations had access to such circuits, in Britain motor racing had never been allowed on the public road and this implacable action by a horse-orientated government stifled development. The best they could manage was a public road course either in Ireland, or on the Isle of Man where their 1904 Gordon Bennett Trial was run.

During the Paris *Salon de l'Automobile* (the Motor Show) of 1904 a group of French manufacturers had mounted an attack upon Gordon Bennett restrictions which was to bring about that competition's downfall and replacement by the Grand Prix.

That inaugural Grand Prix race was eventually held on Tuesday and Wednesday, 26th–27th June 1906, on a mighty 64·12-mile circuit laid out to the east of Le Mans. The temporary

Chargers abroad in the first Grand Prix: Ferenc Szisz's 13-litre 4-cylinder Renault blasts along one of the Le Mans circuit's interminable straights on his way to victory.

facilities were lavish in the extreme, but the road surface itself proved rough as a large field of cars thundered round for six laps on each of the two days. Beneath a blistering sun it became a story of tyre life. The regulations allowed only the driver and riding mechanic to replace worn and punctured tyres and Renault, Itala and Fiat adopted Michelin detachable wheel rims to ease their task. This allowed the old tyre to be removed on its rim once eight bolts had been released. A new tyre, ready-inflated on a replacement rim, could then be bolted on. This device proved crucial as other teams lost time, and energy, hacking off old tyres with knives and replacing them by new tubes and covers which then had to be inflated.

The race was won by Renault's Hungarian-born works test driver, Ferenc Szisz – the pronunciation of whose name has befuddled racing enthusiasts ever since ('Zizz' will do . . .). His 13-litre 90-hp car took the lead on lap three of the first day's racing and held it to the finish despite breaking a spring. He won from the Italian ace Felice Nazzaro in a 16·3-litre 100-hp Fiat, and averaged 62·88 mph for the 768 miles. Fastest race lap was set by Paul Baras' Brasier at 52 min 25·4 sec, an average of 73·3 mph, but despite this vivid demonstration of speed and potential the race was seen as a rather dull battle between Renault and Fiat, with little international significance – remember these were patriotic times – and there was very little 'feeling of sport'.

However, if the very first Grand Prix race had been something less than a total success, there were some very exciting developments afoot, and they had their root, of course, in France, which continued to be the hotbed of motor racing endeavour.

The journal *L'Auto* had revived interest in the voiturette classes, establishing a competition for, as it said so loftily '. . . not merely racing cars' but for roadworthy vehicles limited both by weight and to less than 1 litre in engine size. This limitation was something of a revolution, as manufacturers had formerly been allowed simply to fit the largest possible engine in the flimsiest possible chassis. Interest in what was to become the extremely significant *Coupe de l'Auto* competition was at first minimal, but the event went ahead in November 1905, and was a complete fiasco. The magazine's proprietors stuck to their guns, however, and in 1906 their race at Rambouillet was run for vehicles weighing at least 700 kg (compared to the Grand Prix maximum limit of 1,000 kg) and with the 1-litre engine restriction replaced by a cylinder bore restriction of 120 mm for singles, or 90 mm for twins.

Georges Sizaire won the race in one of his own Sizaire–Naudins, using a 1,357-cc single-cylinder engine delivering all of 18 hp. The winning car featured shaft-drive in place of the heavy chain-drive arrangement favoured by the much larger Grand Prix cars of the day, and many such advanced features were to be developed in this voiturette class within the next few years – features which would quickly change the face of the Grand Prix car itself.

While the *Coupe de l'Auto* regulations changed rapidly, so did those governing what became the annual *Grand Prix de l'ACF*, which had immediately established itself as the most important motor sporting event of its day. Between 1906 and 1908 (when a trade recession caused Grand Prix racing to be abandoned for four years) and 1912–14, the ACF's Grand Prix regulations may be summarised as follows:

1906 1,000 kg (2,205 lb) maximum weight limitation, engine size free.

1907 Fuel consumption allowance of 30 litres (6·6 Imperial galls) per 100 km race distance (62 miles), demanding approximately 9·4 mpg minimum.

1908 Piston area of engines restricted to 117 square inches, equivalent to a 155-mm bore diameter limit for a four-cylinder engine, or a 127-mm limit for a six-cylinder engine.

1912 Grand Prix revived with neither weight nor engine size restrictions.

1913 Fuel consumption allowance reintroduced, this time 20 litres (4·4 Imperial galls) per 100 km (62 miles) race distance, demanding approximately 14·1 mpg. Weight restricted to between 800 and 1,100 kg (1,764–2, 425·5 lb).

1914 A capacity limitation introduced on the swept volume of competing engines, set at 4·5 litres. Weight limited to not more than 1,100 kg (2,425·5 lb).

In its second and third runnings, in 1907–8, the Grand Prix established itself as the annual cynosure of all manufacturers' eyes. Victory in the Grand Prix, as a one-shot 'win or bust' event, could prove of enormous promotional value in a growing motoring market. During the years of weight limitations, engines grew until 12 litres became merely an average displacement. In 1906, Panhard's 130-hp model displaced 18·2 litres, and Dufaux sought dominance with a staggering 26·4-litre, four-cylinder car at one stage! All this for a power output of around 140 hp at less than 2,000 rpm. Today a 3-litre Cosworth–Ford V8 Formula 1 engine delivers some 485 hp at around 11,000 rpm. By this time crews sat in, rather than on, most of the cars as bodyshells grew around them. Dropped chassis frames were adopted to lower the cars' centre of gravity, place the mass of those huge engines closer to the ground, and increase the vehicle's inherent stability.

But all was not well for the French establishment. It was bad enough when Nazzaro's Fiat outpaced Szisz's Renault in 1907 to reverse the inaugural Grand Prix result. This was on the new 47·8-mile circuit near Dieppe, where for the first time trenches were dug alongside the start–finish area to house fuel and spares supplies for the cars – thus coining the term 'pits', which has been in use ever since.

In 1908, when Christian Lautenschlager's Mercedes led home two Benz cars in a German 1–2–3, the pill was so bitter that the proud French could not swallow it. Their best finish was Rigal's Clément-Bayard in fourth place, followed by three more German products – Mercedes, Opel and Benz. The French industry was stunned and since sales slumped in step with a worldwide trade recession the construction of highly specialised Grand Prix cars had become prohibitively expensive. Thus the *GP de l'ACF* was allowed to lapse. This break in one train of development was not mirrored in voiturette racing, where new and dynamic concerns such as Peugeot and Delage were rapidly finding their feet and their efforts ensured that France would maintain its hold on motor racing for a few years longer yet.

Meanwhile, in Britain, the Royal Automobile Club (RAC) had run their first Tourist Trophy race in the Isle of Man in 1905. The entry was deadly dull, being confined strictly to touring cars, but valuable lessons were learned as a Scottish Arrol-Johnston won the first event; Rolls-Royce succeeded in 1906, and Rover took the honours in 1907. International interest was minimal, however, and when an open event was run in 1908 it was won by what was effectively a restyled four-cylinder Napier, running as a Hutton.

British motor racing was in a sadly retarded state. Minor public road sprints and hill-climbs had been held in areas where the squire was enthusiastic and the magistrates were friendly, and the nation's feeble international showings – for few could take the Gordon Bennett success seriously – reflected the lack of high-speed industrial test venues. During 1906, a Weybridge land-

Brooklands introduced the speedway to motor sport but as the years rolled by its concrete bankings settled and became very bumpy. Here in 1936 a bouncing Riley leads a *Monza* Alfa Romeo and a Duesenberg off the Home Banking.

owner named Hugh Fortescue Locke-King began to build just such a test centre on his Brooklands estate. It was a remarkable gesture which cost him £150,000. The Brooklands Motor Course was opened in 1907, as the world's first purpose-built speedway, and with an outer-circuit lap length of 2·75 miles (4·42 km) spectators could watch cars run virtually all the way round.

In its early years, Brooklands had a distinct influence upon the development of vehicle streamlining and racing cars changed shape accordingly – notably with the adoption of long, pointed tail cowls. Thereafter, its rather freakish demands put it out of step with mainstream motor racing, and although a long string of record runs and race meetings were staged there until final closure came in 1939, Brooklands was an oddball venue, demanding highly specialised cars. Towards the end of its life, a road-like infield course was added, but the track gained more significance in the development of British aviation than it did in British motor racing, once an airfield was established in its centre.

Its early lesson was learned particularly well in the USA, however, where the Indianapolis Motor Speedway was built in 1909. Two years later the inaugural Indianapolis 500-Miles Sweepstake race was run, and this extraordinarily well-promoted event survives to this day as the world's richest motor race. Other tracks developed around the Brooklands theme, notably Monza outside

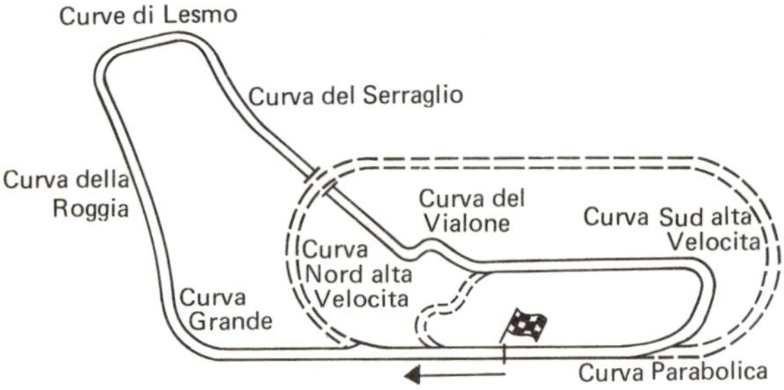

Monza, Italy.

Milan, Italy; Montlhéry near Paris; the Sitges-Terramar autodrome outside Barcelona, Spain; eventually AVUS in Berlin, Germany; and Maroubra bowl in Sydney, Australia. Many American promoters followed the example of Indianapolis, initially with cheaply constructed wooden board speedways, but later with permanent concrete and brick structures. This whole theme was vastly different to mainstream road racing and naturally it was the money-minded Americans who made best use of the potential their speedways afforded. As seems to be the case with so many British innovations, the British themselves had neither the wit nor the money-making drive to make Brooklands so profitable.

Despite the manufacturers' ban on Grand Prix racing in France, a 1909 event was mooted at Anjou. The regulations demanded a minimum entry of forty cars. Only nine entries were made and the event was shelved. The following year rolled by, but then in 1911 the *Automobile Club de la Sarthe* ran a free-Formula *Grand Prix de France* on part of the 1906 Le Mans course.

Victor Hemery won in a modified 10-litre Fiat at 56·71 mph (91·25 kph) but there in second place was Friderich's tiny Bugatti voiturette. The event, although derided by some as the 'Old Crocks Race', goaded the ACF back into action to revive their mighty Grand Prix, and this they did in 1912 at Dieppe.

During these years, voiturette development had continued at such a pace that these small cars had virtually caught up with the traditional Grand Prix machines whose design had congealed four years previously. While the Old Crocks' Race at Le Mans had been interesting in 1911, the year's *Coupe de l'Auto* run on roads outside Boulogne had proved fantastic! Paul Bablot's Delage had beaten Georges Boillot's Lion-Peugeot by only 71 seconds after a seven-hour battle. The lesson was not lost on the ACF committee and to insure against a poor Grand Prix entry for 1912 they ran the race concurrently with the next *Coupe de l'Auto*, which by this time was for 3-litre voiturettes.

Peugeot developed a 7·6-litre shaft-drive model which was a kind of half-way house between their voiturettes and the full blown Grand Prix norm, and entered both Grand Prix and voiturette classes.

The result was a triumph for new over old as Boillot's revolutionary twin overhead camshaft, four-valve per cylinder 'intermediate' Peugeot beat Louis Wagner's old-style 14-litre chain-driven Fiat into second place. But still the French were horrified to see a 1–2–3 *Coupe de l'Auto* success go to Sunbeam, of Britain – Victor Rigal winning in his Brooklands-developed long-tail car from Wolverhampton.

Typically, such shameful trickery as a long streamlined tail

The spirit of Grand Prix racing in its infancy: Louis Wagner's 14-litre chain-drive Fiat hurtles down one of Dieppe's tree-lined straights on its way to second place behind the smaller, shaft-drive Peugeot of Georges Boillot. These monster cars could easily exceed 100 mph yet the spectators on the roadside seem unconcerned.

section was expressly forbidden in the 1913 Grand Prix regulations, when Peugeot won again with Boillot driving. Then came the 1914 race, mere weeks before World War I broke out, which represented perhaps the all-time zenith of Grand Prix racing's significance.

The event was run over 20 laps of a hilly 23·38-mile (37·631-km) circuit at Lyon-Givors and no fewer than fourteen manufacturers entered full teams. Boillot's Peugeot broke after a desperate fight against the Germanic might of Mercedes, and Christian Lautenschlager led home two team-mates to a German 1–2–3 finish – received in stoney silence by the Gallic crowd. It was the end of an era: as war engulfed Europe, Grand Prix engine technology was used in aviation's battle, and both Peugeot and Mercedes found a racing refuge in America.

Racing Between the Wars

Mainstream motor racing burned steadily through the 1920s, stumbled and virtually died during the Great Depression and flared to a white-heat of technical and political significance in the middle and late 1930s.

As early as 1919, road racing recommenced, in the incredible Targa Florio event run on public 'roads' among the Madonie Mountains of northern Sicily. André Boillot – younger brother of the great Georges Boillot who had died flying in World War I – won the race for Peugeot. An Italian named Antonio Ascari led the opening stages before crashing heavily in his pre-war Grand Prix Fiat.

Racing was revived by American influence. The USA had remained untouched by the war, its speedway facilities were intact and its years as a belligerent in 1917–18 had forced technological development in a mirror image of what had happened in Europe. Aero-engine developments were particularly significant: eight-cylinder power units were now to replace the four-cylinder units which had maintained a stranglehold pre-war; and through 1919–20 notably Duesenberg and the French Ballot concern met head-on in American track racing with their straight-eight designs.

In 1921, the *Grand Prix de l'ACF* was revived on a new 10·726-mile (17·262 km) circuit at Le Mans. The American 3-litre capacity Formula was adopted and the Ballots were beaten by Duesenberg, running their products in Europe on a shoe-string budget.

The 1920s were to see the proliferation of Grand Prix style racing. Whereas pre-World War I there had been only one, extremely important, Grand Prix race each year, now others were to join the French event in an international calendar. Italy's first Grand Prix was held at Brescia in 1921 and a pair of Ballots humbled the home team of straight-eight Fiats. Monza Autodrome was opened in the Royal Park outside Milan in 1922, and became the home of the national Grand Prix thereafter. In 1924, a Spanish race was added at San Sebastian – although it was not accorded *Grande Epreuve* (Great Test) status by the French-dominated international governing body of the sport. A Belgian Grand Prix was inaugurated in 1925, and in 1926 the first British and German Grands Prix were organised. In Britain the Tourist Trophy (TT) had long since been revived, but its international significance was still limited.

During the early 1920s, inter-marque rivalry was fierce and furious in a 2-litre Formula. The Formulae in use between the world wars may be summarised as follows:

1921	3-litre capacity – minimum weight of 800 kg (1,764 lb).
1922–4	2-litre capacity – minimum weight of 650 kg (1,433·25 lb).
1925	2-litre capacity limit continued but riding mechanics banned after a series of accident casualties. Wide two-seat body styles still mandatory; rear-view mirrors (replacing a riding mechanic's eyes) introduced.
1926	1½-litre capacity – minimum weight of 600 kg (1,323 lb), single-seats allowed, set within full-width bodyshells as before.
1927	1½-litre capacity limit continued but minimum weight now raised to 700 kg (1,543·5 lb).
1928	Engines free with minimum weight decided on a sliding scale from 550 kg (1,212·75 lb) and 750 kg (1,653·75 lb) relative to engine capacity. Minimum race distance demanded was 600 km (362 miles).
1929	Commercial petrol mandatory in place of exotic fuel brews, with a consumption limit of approximately 14·5 mpg.
1930	As above but with a concession to allow 30 per cent benzol to be added to commercial fuel.
1931	Free Formula – races to last a minimum of 10 hours.
1932	Free Formula – races to last between 5 and 10 hours.

1933	Free Formula – race distance to be a minimum of 500 km (312 miles).
1934–6	Maximum weight limit of 750 kg (1,653·75 lb) as measured excluding water, oil, fuel and tyres.
1937	Formula extended for one extra season.
1938	3-litre capacity limit for supercharged engines with 4½-litre capacity limit for unsupercharged engines. Minimum weight limit of 850 kg (1,874 lb) with a sliding weight scale for intermediate engine capacities.

Those 2-litre Formula years in the early 1920s saw Fiat dominant in 1922, winning both the Italian and ACF Grands Prix. The French race fell to Felice Nazzaro's car – as it had in 1907 – and the 8·3-mile (13·38-km) circuit at Strasbourg was interesting in being very fast, and so short. The race witnessed the first massed-start in place of the old '30-second interval between pairs' departure, and it was the last Grand Prix in which spare wheels were carried on the cars. This was partly a move by the organisers to stimulate tyre development, but also reflected the development of pit-work and the shorter lap distance contributing towards the riding mechanic becoming redundant.

The year's victorious Fiat *Tipo* 804s were six-cylinder models and Louis Coatalen – Breton chief engineer of the British Sunbeam company – had them faithfully copied to produce a 'Fiat in Green Paint' which carried Major H. O. D. Segrave to victory in the 1923 French Grand Prix at Tours. By this time Fiat had produced the supercharged straight-eight *Tipo* 805 model, but though shatteringly fast it ingested dust and stones into its supercharger intake and failed. However, on home ground at Monza, the cars were not to be denied.

Alfa Romeo, the rival Italian marque, promptly hired Fiat's leading engineers and had them produce the racing P2 model for 1924, and promptly humbled Fiat on the sacred surface at Monza!

This period also saw Fiat and the Sunbeam–Talbot–Darracq combine heavily engaged in 1½-litre voiturette racing – using what was effectively one-half of their 1921 3-litre straight-eight cylin-

Grid start of the French GP at Lyon in 1924 with Segrave's Sunbeam hurtling away from Ascari's Alfa Romeo and Guinness's sister Sunbeam. The huge scoreboard kept the massed crowd informed of progress through the seven hour race.

der racing engine design. Fiat ruled the roost in Italy with their cars, while the French-built Talbots won every race they entered elsewhere in Europe, earning themselves the title 'The Invincibles' between 1921 and 1925.

In 1926 the Grand Prix Formula changed to elevate the former 1½-litre voiturette class to premier league status. During 1925 Alfa Romeo and the daring French Delage company had shared the honours in an interesting Grand Prix season and an under-publicised World Championship awarded by the governing body (the *Association Internationale des Automobile Clubs Reconnus* – AIACR) had gone narrowly to the Italian marque.

The new Formula was contested by Delage, Talbot and Bugatti, but the S–T–D combine ran out of money, leaving the troublesome Delages to play second-fiddle to Bugatti in 1926, then crush them totally in 1927.

Trade was entering those harrowing years of the Great Depression and by 1928 the major factory teams had withdrawn, private owners formed the backbone of international race entries and sports car events gained importance.

The idea of using vehicles in competition which were more practical than the thoroughbred Grand Prix car had been typified by the staid early days of the British TT event, but sports car racing as it developed owed more to the German 'trials' held from 1905 to 1911. Professor Hubert von Herkomer, RA (a portrait painter) devised his International Touring Car Competition in 1905 when it was contested by ordinary production models, tackling a 500 miles road test followed by a hill-climb and brief speed trial. In 1906, cars were entered with lightweight streamlined bodies and high-performance engines. One driver was Prince Henry of Prussia, the Kaiser's younger brother, and when the last Herkomer Trial was completed in 1907 he launched his own *Prinz Heinrich* Trophy which attracted some very advanced and potent 'sporting cars' based on production models. Austro-Daimler, with a Dr Ferdinand Porsche-designed car, and Vauxhall profited notably from this experience.

After 1911, the well-established Austrian Alpine Trial took over the Prince Henry Trial's mantle as a stimulating challenge for the promotions-minded manufacturer of the time whose ambitions fell just short of Grand Prix racing.

After World War I, 24-hour racing was brought to Europe from America, where 'The Grind' had proved a popular speedway attraction from early on. The first 24-hour *Bol d'Or was* run with a minimum of organisation at St Germain in 1922. Almost anything on wheels was allowed to start, and the winner was André Morel in an 1,100-cc Amilcar, having averaged 37·54 mph (60·4 kph) for the duration. In 1923, the Le Mans club launched their far more significant endeavour, the famous 24-Hour *Grand Prix d'Endurance*. Like the old-established TT it began as a touring car event, and on 26th–27th May 1923 Lagache and Leonard won the maiden race in a 3-litre Chenard et

Walcker; covering 1,372·9 miles (2,209 km) at an average speed of 57·2 mph (92 kph). They used a new 10·726-mile (17·26-km) course to the south of the French industrial city, and it is on a modified version of this circuit that the famous Le Mans 24-Hours race is still run today.

In Italy, a remarkable throwback to the old city-to-city era occurred in 1927 when Renzo Castagneto and Count Aymo Maggi launched their 1,000-mile Mille Miglia – starting and finishing at Brescia after looping right around the 'boot' of Italy. Alfa Romeo dominated the event, while Bentley cars made their reputation at Le Mans, winning five times from 1924 to 1930. The British TT died after 1922 but was revived on Ulster's Ards circuit in 1928, but as a handicap race it may have equalised small and large car entries but nullified its international appeal.

Tazio Nuvolari hurls his Alfa Romeo past the tribunes in the 1932 Targa Florio in Sicily – this magnificent motor race surviving little changed until 1977.

With the onset of the Depression, sports cars were raced at all levels, often even in Grand Prix events where with lights and mudguards removed they could give a good account of themselves – as in 1930 when Tim Birkin's Bentley was second in the French Grand Prix. In later years, as the German teams of Mercedes-Benz and Auto Union dominated Grand Prix racing, the French actually demoted their Grand Prix to sports car status just to give their own manufacturers a chance to win.

The Depression years saw Free Formula, or *Formule Libre*, racing keep the Grand Prix tradition alive. In 1930, Maserati emerged to win five major events with a 2½-litre supercharged straight-eight design. Bugatti fought back with a twin-cam Type 51 model in 1931, and then Mussolini's Fascist regime in Italy supported Alfa Romeo as they introduced their classical centrally-disposed, single-seat *Monoposto* model in 1932 and swept all before them.

In 1933, the AIACR recognised that industry was emerging from the world recession, and that it was time to impose a proper Grand Prix Formula once more. The years of *Formule Libre* racing had produced some fearsome big-engined monsters which had sent race speeds rocketing and as always sheer speed was to be restricted and limitations were to be imposed – for the sake of safety. They announced the 750-kilogramme Formula to take effect from 1st January 1934, and this was a *maximum* weight limit intended to outlaw over-powered freak cars and to encourage the development of more modest designs.

Unfortunately for the French-dominated legislators, the German Nazi regime had recognised the lesson of Mussolin's support for Alfa Romeo – and the national prestige their motor racing success had brought to Italy. With state backing, Mercedes-Benz and Auto Union produced formidable Grand Prix designs making extensive use of light-alloys, adopting streamlined body forms, all-independent suspension systems, powerful hydraulic brakes and rapidly growing (but still well within the weight limit) engines of unmatched power. Initially these teams employed the best available international drivers while training their home-grown talent and after some early setbacks Mercedes-Benz and Auto Union dominated 1930s Grand Prix racing with total self-assurance. By 1937 the 750-kg Formula had produced the most powerful Grand Prix cars ever seen, with a gross power output still unmatched today! Mercedes' M125 engine – which was a straight-eight supercharged unit of 5·66 litres capacity – could produce 646 bhp, compared to today's 3-litre Ferrari flat-12s at '510 bhp'. Auto Union's 6-litre supercharged V16-cylinder engine was barely less potent. These cars could attain a genuine 200 mph on some circuits which could accommodate such high speeds and with minimal attention to trackside safety (hedges, ditches, trees and telegraph poles were common obstacles), still narrow wheel rims and marginal tyres and braking capability, they were unimaginably challenging to drive. Whereas a modern Formula 1 car might be unable to

The German Age in 1937 when Mercedes-Benz and Auto Union produced the most powerful GP cars the world has ever seen. Here at Donington Park Bernd Rosemeyer won with this tricky-to-handle mid-engined Auto Union. Behind his shoulders is a V16-cylinder 6-litre engine punching 590 bhp through those rear wheels.

exceed 180 mph in a straight line it can corner at perhaps 160 mph with ease. In similar conditions the 1937 car might run beyond 190 mph on the straight – being a more slippery shape without the drag of wings and wide tyres – but it would be unable to negotiate the same corner at more than 100 mph; a fairly desperate braking manoeuvre is indicated.

Not for nothing the men who drove those cars – Caracciola, Brauchitsch, Rosemeyer, Lang and Seaman among them – were nicknamed 'The Titans'.

In 1938 a swingeing Formula change was made to cut this escalation in speed and power. From a *maximum* weight allowance of 750 kg and unlimited engine sizes, 1938–40 cars were restricted to a *minimum* weight of 850 kg with supercharged engines of no more than 3 litres capacity. Unsupercharged engines were allowed an extra 1½ litres to total 4½ litres capacity, but in practice Grand Prix racing was still no contest as the twin-stage supercharged German cars of 1939 began to threaten 1937 standards of lap time and outright speed.

The French, left only with Bugatti, Delahaye and Talbot-Lago racing, had quickly fallen back upon sports car competition to maintain some semblance of respectability. The Italians fought longer to remain competitive with their Axis partner, but by 1938 Alfa Romeo and Maserati spent more time fighting each other in 1½-litre supercharged voiturette racing. This was a class in which the British ERA team had excelled, using six-cylinder Riley-based engines in the mid-1930s, but in which they were now outpaced by the Italian teams. Then at Tripoli in 1939, Mercedes-Benz made a one-off entry with a special 1½-litre V8 version of their Grand Prix design which flayed the Italians mercilessly – two of these W165s leading home one surviving Alfa Romeo . . . by a margin of over four minutes!

This remarkable period of accelerated development was halted abruptly on 3rd September 1939, when World War II broke out in Europe. The great Italian driver, Tazio Nuvolari, fittingly won the last Grand Prix race, in Belgrade, Yugoslavia, a few hours after Britain's declaration of war on Germany. Of course, he was driving a German car – an Auto Union.

During these inter-war years circuits had grown shorter, though still predominantly consisting of closed public roads. Paying crowds had grown larger, the cars they saw proved enormously faster and the sport had become established not merely as an instrument of commercial promotion and technical development, but also as one of political prestige. Italy raced on into 1940 as she remained neutral from the war, and Alfa Romeo, Mercedes-Benz and Auto Union all had 1½-litre supercharged Grand Prix designs ready for a new Formula optimistically expected for 1941. As it was, the German and Italian industries had their minds concentrated elsewhere by that time.

Racing Towards Today

As Europe emerged from its second great war, mainstream motor racing was quick to recommence. Just one week after the Japanese surrender was signed in Tokyo Bay, the French ran the first postwar circuit race, in the Bois de Boulogne park in Paris, on 9th September 1945.

In Italy, work began to revive the Alfa Romeo and Maserati voiturettes which had ruled their national roost so thoroughly in prewar days. During 1946 there were seventeen major race meetings in Europe, run mainly on town circuits, easily accessible to a public deprived of private transport.

The cars and drivers which did the winning all bore familiar names from the 1930s, like Nuvolari, Varzi, Count Trossi, Dr Farina, Raymond Sommer and Wimille – the latter rapidly becoming the man to beat in his private Alfa Romeo 308 and factory-entered Alfa 158s.

Britain had lost the Brooklands Track, and the road circuits which had been established on private land in the 1930s, such as Donington Park and Crystal Palace, had yet to reopen. Competition quickly resumed on the short hill-climb venues like Shelsley Walsh and Prescott, which had assumed major national stature before the war. But even they could never compare with the immense mountain climb courses of Europe, in which even

Mercedes-Benz and Auto Union had seen fit to dabble.

The lack of artificial road circuits persuaded a hard-core of British enthusiasts to experiment with airfield racing around the perimeter tracks of the numerous disused aerodromes which now littered their country. On 15th June 1946, the first, prophetic, airfield race was run at Gransden Lodge aerodrome by the Cambridge University Auto Club and Reg Parnell won the feature event with his 16-valve Maserati.

The RAC noted the experiment, and after closed public road circuit races had been run successfully in the Isle of Man and Ulster, they opened their own Silverstone airfield circuit with the revived British Grand Prix race of 1948.

Meanwhile, 1947 had seen the major Swiss, Belgian and Italian

For nine years after World War II, GP cars tended still to be pre-war in design. Here Louis Rosier demonstrates his style in the 4½-litre unsupercharged French Talbot-Lago. Compare this with jet aircraft of the late '40s and a technology gap becomes apparent!

Grands Prix revived in Europe, and the works team of *Alfetta* voiturettes did the winning, picking up in Grand Prix racing where they had been forced to stop in the 1½-litre class in 1940. The old AIACR governing body was reconstituted as the *Federation Internationale de l'Automobile* (FIA) and announced that it would enforce a new 1½-litre supercharged Grand Prix Formula from 1948, which would also cater for unsupercharged cars of up to 4½ litres. This was totally logical, as the great German teams had been shattered and scattered by the war and this announcement merely formalised a status quo with predominantly Italian supercharged voiturettes racing against predominantly French unsupercharged 4½-litre models from Talbot-Lago.

Technical development was virtually frozen in the 1939-mould by this move, and the larger disparity between the small (and fuel thirsty) supercharged cars and the larger, slower, but less thirsty '4½s' was to provide better balanced racing than had the 3-litre supercharged class of 1938–9. While the reliable unsupercharged cars could cover a 500-km (312-mile) Grand Prix distance non-stop, the blown 1½s were much faster but had to stop once and sometimes twice to refuel. This provided quite exciting tortoise-and-the-hare style racing, but the 4½s could never approach the pace (pit stops included) of the factory Alfa Romeo team cars when they ran.

Alfa, Maserati, the new Ferrari outfit (founded by Enzo Ferrari who had run Alfa's prewar teams) and some aged British ERAs faced the unsupercharged Talbot-Lago.

Racing progressed until 1950 when the FIA instituted their World Drivers' Championship, which more than any other competition has rivetted the attention of the general public. There was a Constructors' Championship, too, but the personality competition attracted the media more than the nuts and bolts. As years rolled by, so major motor manufacturers slipped away from Grand Prix racing as the names of the men in the cockpits took precedence over their trade titles. Instead they turned their attention towards endurance racing, and rallying – like the Le Mans 24-Hours classic and the Monte Carlo Rally.

The Grand Prix Formula which had been applied in 1948 was intended to run through 1953, but after Ferrari turned to building unsupercharged $4\frac{1}{2}$-litre V12 cars and humbled Alfa Romeo in terms of reliable and economic pace, the historic Italian marque withdrew – with the first two World Championship titles to their name for Giuseppe Farina and Juan-Manuel Fangio. The British BRM team were struggling to race-develop their ambitious V16 $1\frac{1}{2}$-litre supercharged design and since they could not guarantee entries against Ferrari, Formula 1 – as the Grand Prix class was now known – it simply died on its feet.

Since 1948, an unsupercharged 2-litre voiturette class had been established, known initially as Formula B (when the Grand Prix class had been known as Formula A) and later as Formula 2. At the end of 1951 the FIA allowed Grand Prix race organisers to open their World Championship events to Formula 2 cars and the result was two seasons (1952–3) of total Ferrari domination as the Maranello team's lead driver, Alberto Ascari, won consecutive World Championship titles. He was the son of the great Alfa Romeo ace Antonio Ascari, who had crashed fatally while leading the 1925 French Grand Prix at Montlhéry.

A new Formula 1 was announced to come into effect in 1954, and this effectively restarted technical development postwar and was to force lap and race speeds beyond their 1934–9 levels. It demanded unsupercharged engines of not more than $2\frac{1}{2}$-litres capacity, with supercharged units restricted to only 750 cc. Weight was free, and the might of Mercedes-Benz returned to the fray in face of Maserati, Ferrari, Lancia and the British Connaught, HWM, Cooper and Vanwall teams.

The postwar upsurge in British motor racing was enormous and dynamic. The expensive BRM V16 project, although a failure, had sparked interest on a massive scale. From 1946 a 'poor man's motor racing' movement had grown, using 500-cc motorcycle engines in a stark, single-seater chassis. The Cooper Car Company run by Charles Cooper and his son John grew to dominate this class which attained international recognition as Formula 3. In this Britain had herself the most effective racing driver training school in the world, and men like Stirling Moss and Peter Collins were its graduates. Other shoe-string companies sprang up, and sports car racing flourished. British chassis design was remarkably effective and production companies like Jaguar recognised the promotional value of events such as Le Mans and set about winning the race five times – as had Bentley before them.

A World Sports Car Championship instituted in 1953 had become largely a Ferrari preserve although its endurance rounds were disputed by such prestigious names as Mercedes-Benz, Lancia, Maserati, Aston Martin and Jaguar during the 1950s. That decade saw sports cars develop from open cockpit roadsters, which could be driven to and from the circuits on the public road, into highly specialised purebred racing machines impracticable for normal road use.

Britain revived production car racing at Silverstone in 1949 when the BRDC and the *Daily Express* newspaper organised a One Hour race. Jaguar fielded three XK120s, painted red, white and blue, to dominate the race, but the crowd loved the antics of ordinary road cars pursuing the sports models. Visiting Europeans spread the production car gospel on the Continent, and by the early 1960s a complicated European Touring Car Challenge was initiated, subdivided by engine capacity and producing a European Touring Car Champion Driver rather than manufacturer. This developed into the European Touring Car Championship for manufacturers, with names like Ford, BMW and Alfa Romeo locked in combat. For a short time in the early 1970s, million pound budgets were poured into the series by publicity-hungry manufacturers.

Meanwhile Grand Prix racing had undergone tremendous change. In 1955, a professional dentist and part-time racing driver named Tony Brooks had won the non-Championship Syracuse Grand Prix in Sicily for the under-financed Connaught team. It was the first British car/driver success in a European Grand Prix race since Segrave's victory for Sunbeam at San Sebastian, Spain in 1924! Thus encouraged, British interest blossomed, and the Vanwall team run by industrialist G. A. 'Tony' Vandervell showed remarkable pace in 1956. By 1957 they added reliability and with the services of Moss and Brooks (now professional) they began to win World Championship events.

Juan-Manuel Fangio accumulated five World Championship titles during this period, with his last (for Maserati) in 1957, but the wind of change was blowing strongly.

In 1958, Formula 1 was modified to demand the use of 100-octane AvGas aviation petrol in place of special chemical fuels, and race distance was cut from three hours or 500 km to only two hours or 300 km (180 miles) duration. Cooper had developed 2-litre Formula 2 versions of their successful and simple mid-engined design, using lightweight Coventry Climax proprietary engines, developed originally from a fire-pump power unit. With

John Surtees' 1964 Ferrari leaps high on its way to victory in the German GP at Nürburgring.

shorter races, the nimble little Coopers could run nonstop without suffering a fuel capacity handicap, and when full 2½-litre Climax engines became available, they put the larger and less manoeuvrable front-engined cars to flight. Australian driver Jack Brabham brought Cooper the World Championships in 1959 and 1960, when the fast-rising Lotus team, BRM and Ferrari all produced their own mid-engined models.

Their approach was more scientific than Cooper's, and when a 1½-litre unsupercharged Formula 1 was imposed from 1961 to 1965 it was Lotus and BRM – using British multi-cylinder engines – who dominated the class, winning three world titles with Graham Hill and Jimmy Clark while Ferrari stole two for Phil Hill and John Surtees.

Within three brief seasons in the late 1950s the centre of the motor racing world had shifted from Italy to Britain, where specialist chassis-building teams used off-the-shelf engines and transmissions supplied by specialists. Only Ferrari and BRM of the regular runners were left building their own chassis, engines and gearboxes, and the new era of the Formula 1 'special builders' had arrived.

The 1½-litre Formula 1 years saw close and still quite fast racing, but in general the cars were, by common consent, too easy to drive. When negotiations began with the FIA for the new Formula due in 1966 the British manufacturers got together and figured that a 2-litre class would be ideal since they could develop their existing engines without the expensive tooling and redesign and development necessary for all-new equipment. Knowing the FIA's cautious tendency to err on the side of safety and restricted performance, they decided to suggest a 3-litre unsupercharged category, sure that the legislators would compromise on 2 litres. Imagine the British delegation's amazement when the authorities agreed that 3 litres would be perfect, and announced the new Formula accordingly! It was a classic case of 'back to the drawing board'.

This 3-litre Formula in constantly revised form has been with us ever since and it has become by far the longest-lived Formula in the history of Grand Prix racing. It has seen the development

A classic Formula 1 race start, in this instance for the non-Championship Brands Hatch Race of Champions in 1967. Fastest qualifier and so on pole position (nearest the camera) is Dan Gurney's Eagle, with team-mate Richie Ginther's second car next-up flanked by Surtees' Japanese Honda. Behind are Ludovico Scarfiotti's Ferrari and Pedro Rodriguez's Cooper-Maserati.

of the most all-embracing set of regulations in GP history, the most basic changes ever in the public face of the sport and some of the most prolific, best-supported, most competitive and fastest Grand Prix racing ever experienced.

While it was quite common in the 1950s for a dozen Grand Prix cars to set off on a 312-mile Championship race, the 3-litre Formula has witnessed as many as 35 cars tackling qualification for a 32-car grid to start a 250 km (155 miles) race of about 90 minutes' duration. This recipe has been packaged and sold to the nations of western Europe, to North America, South America, and even to Japan and has proved immensely successful in both crowd attraction and its associated financial reward.

In 1966, there were nine World Championship-qualifying

Grands Prix, and in 1977 there were 17. The one-time crop of very enjoyable but insignificant non-Championship races has been stamped out by the commercial interests of the British-dominated Formula 1 circus. Most of these teams rely on the Ford of Dagenham-financed Cosworth DFV 3-litre V8 engine and the introduction of this unit for Team Lotus's exclusive use in 1967 and its subsequent release for general F1 sale in 1968 was a decisive factor in producing near uniformity of performance and extreme competitiveness in the class.

Meanwhile a fiercely-fought tyre war between Dunlop, Goodyear and Firestone which had started in 1964 reached its climax in the early years of the 3-litre Formula. Dunlop surrendered, having been stifled by America's big money approach, in 1970 and Firestone pulled out in 1974 to leave Goodyear with a monopoly. Forced tyre development sent lap and race speeds soaring, and the development of highly specialised wet and dry-weather tyres escalated all-round costs to soak up more commercial sponsorship money.

In 1977 a new trend may have begun as the state-backed French Renault company became the first to take advantage of the 1½-litre supercharged engine section of the Formula 1 regulations, and they fitted an exhaust-driven turbocharger to a V6 engine proven in sports-racing and Formula 2 cars and mounted it in a neat single-seat F1 chassis. Using Michelin tyres from another important French concern, they felt their way carefully into Grand Prix racing and as Michelin tyres appeared on Ferrari cars in 1978 the prospects for another tyre war and further forced development looked bright. Renault had won the very first Grand Prix race in 1906, and their attempts to make the wheel come full circle to win again in the 1970s is being closely watched by other major motor manufacturers. The day of the 'special builders' – although their latest products have been very sophisticated – may well be approaching its end.

2 Racing as a Science

Each year sees the *Federation Internationale de l'Automobile* issue what is known as 'The Yellow Book'; actually the *FIA Year Book of Automobile Sport*. It is published in bilingual English/French form by Patrick Stephens Ltd, and in something over 400 pages it presents the multitude of rules and regulations which govern every branch of the sport at international level. It details the constructional requirements for every competing car and defines safety standards for motor racing circuits, the regulations governing every international championship and follows up with lists of organising club addresses, circuit and hill-climb venue maps, even data on car manufacturers, engine tuning outfits, the world's motoring press and so on virtually *ad infinitum*. It is only a small-format pocket-book but it is the 'bible' by which every race organiser, team manager and racing car designer pursues his business.

To understand the Formula 1 cars which contest World Championship Grand Prix racing, it is necessary to study the regulations governing their construction. Some of the so-called General Prescriptions concerning Formula 1 apply equally to the minor Formulae 2 and 3, and it is all set down – sometimes rather quaintly in the translation from the FIA's original French-language draft – in 'The Yellow Book'.

Basically, International Formula No. 1 demands reciprocating piston engines of a capacity equal or inferior to 3,000 cc without supercharging, or equal or inferior to 1,500 cc if supercharged by any means.

There is now a maximum cylinder limitation of 12 which places

Typical paddock scene at any 1970s Grand Prix, in this case with the McLaren team cars under preparation. Advertising slogans, choice of tyres and expensive transport equipment all abound.

any further 16-cylinder nonsenses such as the 1966–7 H16 BRM out of court.

Turbine engines are permitted, on the basis of a very complex equation designed to give them equivalency with conventional Formula 1 piston engines.

Minimum weight, without ballast, must be 575 kg (1,268 lb).

Bodywork dimensions are closely prescribed, with an overall maximum width behind the front wheels and extending to the leading edge of the rear wheels of not more than 140 cm. No oil, fuel or electrical lines may be situated further outboard than 60 cm from the car's centreline, neither must they run adjacent to the car's main fuel cells, nor within the crushable impact pads which protect the outer faces of the cells. Oil radiators are not governed by the oil pipe regulation.

Additional restrictions confine the rear overhang (measured

from the rearmost face of the rear wheels) to 80 cm, while the front overhang (from the forward face of the front wheels) must not exceed 120 cm. Maximum width of the complete rear wheel must not exceed 21 inches (measured in Imperial units since rim sizes are largely decided by the tyres the Goodyear tyre company produced during its monopoly years of 1975–6). Rear wheel diameter is limited to 13 inches, while front wheel sizes are free within a maximum overall width of 21 inches. The overall width of the car is limited to 215 cm, measured across the outside extremities of its wheels at the widest end – usually the rear. Rear wing maximum width is prescribed as 110 cm.

Safety features, such as the tank protecting 'deformable structure' pads on either side of the central chassis, roll-over bars erected at the dash panel and behind the driver's head and a foot-pedal box capable of withstanding a 25G (twenty-five times the force of gravity) deceleration without displacing the pedals backwards by more than 150 mm (when the car has a full fuel load and its driver on board) are mandatory. Rubber bladder fuel cells are specified, and they must 'be situated within the main structure of the car', protected by crushable structures not less than 10 mm thick. The fuel system has to be arranged 'so that no part of it is the first object to be struck in an accident' and aviation-style breakaway fuel line couplings are used which self-seal when pulled apart.

Total fuel capacity is limited to 250 litres, of which not more than 80 litres in a single cell, new-type cells apart.

Additional safety features include a clearly indicated external emergency handle which can simultaneously activate the mandatory onboard fire extinguisher system, cut off the engine and isolate the battery, when actuated by emergency personnel. It must be designed so that it can be fired from a distance by a hook if necessary. A driver headrest has to be fitted which is capable of restraining 17 kg under a rearward acceleration of 5G, designed in such a way that it is impossible for the driver's head to become trapped between the headrest and the adjacent roll-over bar.

As an extra fire-safety measure, the use of magnesium sheet in the car will be allowed only if its thickness exceeds 3 mm.

Oversteer: Fittipaldi's tail-sliding Lotus 72 flickers on to corrective left-hand steering lock as it hurtles through a tight right-hand corner. The downthrust effect of the rear wing is balanced up front by the car's wedge-profiled nose and the trim vanes on either side.

The energy source carried on board must be capable of starting the engine at least twice.

Chromium plating of steel suspension members of over 45 tons per square inch tensile strength is forbidden – since it may camouflage evidence of fatigue cracks and incipient breakage.

These then are the Formula 1 prescriptions in essence to which each team's designer builds his car. Today, the Cosworth-Ford DFV V8 engine is the mainstay of Formula 1, with a majority of cars using it mated to Hewland Engineering's highly-developed and reliable transmissions. Ferrari have more power in the horizontally-opposed 'flat-12' cylinder engines which they use and do not make available to outside teams, while Alfa Romeo have a similar power unit developed in sports car racing and in Brabham Formula 1 chassis. Matra provide a V12-cylinder engine to the French Ligier team and Renault are alone – at the time of writing – in taking the 1½-litre supercharged engine option. Their 1,500-cc V6 power unit has an exhaust-driven turbocharger supplying pressurised air to the induction system. As yet, it is still in its experimental stages, but much is expected of it. Ferrari and Alfa Romeo both have turbocharged engines waiting in the wings and other major manufacturers may follow Renault's lead.

Other than their motive power, the restrictive nature of the Formula 1 regulations and the intense pressure of a 17-race World Championship season gravitate towards the construction of simple and basically similar chassis.

The object of the chassis and its attached suspension and aerodynamic aids is to form the most efficient compromise in terms of competitive lap times around a circuit. The expression 'lap times' is all-important, for a road circuit lap is not entirely dependent upon outright straightline speed. On the contrary, the fastest car on a straight may be desperately slow in lap times, for there are corners to be braked into in the shortest possible time; corners to be negotiated at the highest possible speed; and corners to be accelerated out of at the maximum possible rate. To produce a car which performs all these functions is to compromise its efficiency in performing each one, and it is the most efficient compromise which will be rapid and successful.

The final arbiter of lap time in modern motor racing is the performance of the tyre contact patch in touch with the track surface, and the ability of the car's aerodynamics and suspension design to make best use of that patch. The tyre tread in contact with the roadway transmits not only power to provide acceleration, but also braking reaction to slow the car and lateral force which makes it go round corners.

In his early days of international racing James Hunt was convinced that straightline speed was the answer to his problems. 'Give me a car that's faster than the rest down the straight', he said to Hesketh designer Harvey Postlethwaite, '. . . and I'll block 'em all off into the corners!'

In practice, the right answer involves rather more sophisticated engineering. In a race, the track surface is one 'constant', with a grip coefficient which is the same for all concerned, although that coefficient may change dramatically during a race and may even vary from yard to yard. Nevertheless, its nature is common to all who race upon it.

Then there is the tyre, whose coefficient of friction is decided by its design and construction and by the ability of the suspension system which controls it to introduce an optimum working temperature. In a corner, any car drifts imperceptibly while its wheels turn more than one might think absolutely necessary in order to negotiate the turn. The difference between the car's direction of travel and that of its tyres is described as the 'slip angle', and for each given tyre design there is an optimum slip angle, which yields the greatest tyre performance. If a car throws its tail wide while cornering, this is described as 'oversteer', and if it tends to plough straight on the condition is known as 'understeer'. In the USA drivers talk of a car being 'loose' or of it 'pushing' and they mean the same thing.

Equally, oversteer and understeer may be explained in terms of slip-angle; a car oversteering when its rear tyres adopt a greater slip angle than the front, and understeering if the front slip angle is greater than the rear. In either case the tyres on the offending axle have exceeded their optimum slip angle and their frictional performance has fallen-off. They have 'broken away'.

Racing tyres are extremely specialised items. In Goodyear's case, during their years of monopoly, tyres were built up on a man-made textile 'cross-ply' system with treads and sidewalls moulded on to the carcass in a wide range of chemical synthetic rubber mixtures. The precise design of the tyre's carcass construction has a great effect upon its rigidity and response. It is the rubber chemist's job to provide a tread compound which offers optimum grip combined with long-life (or long-enough!) to survive a full race distance; or in the case of endurance racing, a full between-stops distance. Slick tyres with a smooth tread are used in dry conditions, since they place the maximum possible rubber area in contact with the road surface. Grooved treads appear for

The name of the Grand Prix game for many years: tyres and their wheels await union before the Firestone service vans. This American company was eventually crushed in Formula 1 by its larger rival, Goodyear.

rainy conditions, where water has to be siphoned away from the contact patch to enable the tread compound to come into contact with the track surface. While a dry tread compound's optimum operating temperature may be quite high, wet tyres have to achieve their correct operating level while being constantly water-cooled. Effectively, therefore, dry tyre compounds are 'hard' and wet compounds 'soft' so, when a dry slick runs into water, not only does it aquaplane easily (since there are no drainage channels to remove the water from between contact patch and roadway) but it also falls below its most efficient temperature, thereby losing grip in any case. Conversely, a wet tyre run into dry conditions will rapidly overheat and its tread covering will quite literally melt, leaving the car to corner as best it can while laying down broad stripes of gooey compound on the road surface.

Intermediate standard tyres, sufficiently versatile to operate acceptably in changeable weather, have been made but as a compromise they fall short of a specialised tyre's outright performance.

Tyre overloading is a clue to suspension maladjustment, and probe thermometers are used to check tread temperatures across their width during testing or practice. Higher temperature on one side than another indicates a potential problem, and with today's predominantly right-turn road circuits the left-front tyre suffers a particularly heavy loading – not necessarily through suspension maladjustment, but purely because the car is leaning heavily on it for most of the time! Therefore, a team may find it advantageous to fit a harder tyre on one corner than on the others.

If a new tyre is punished too heavily, too quickly, its critical tread compound temperature may be exceeded and blisters will appear and burst. If this occurs in a race all is lost, for a change must in most cases be made. Heavy cars, unsympathetically-driven cars and badly set-up cars may burn-out their tyres (particularly at the front) in a less abrupt manner. This phenomenon, known as 'graining' or 'feathering', rolls little pieces of rubber off the tread – diminishing its grip. A watchful driver will recognise the condition as one edge of his front tyres – or of the rears seen in his mirrors – will blacken. The car's cornering power will be limited and if he presses on the condition will worsen. A sensitive driver will ease off, roll-away the loose granulation, and after a few laps will see his tyres regain their normal appearance and will find much of their adhesion restored.

Similarly the appearance of the front tyres may provide a driver with his first warning that oil or moisture is beginning to coat the track surface, as they take on a rather sinister, glossy sheen.

At top level, the standards of tyres fitted are all-important. They make the difference between winning and losing and so intense attention is paid to them. Occasionally badly-made tyres will appear which are misshapen or fractionally oversize. Just a few millimetres discrepancy on overall diameter makes a marked difference to the tyre's rolling circumference, and this inequality with another tyre on the same axle will make a pig of a perfectly-adjusted racing car. If the driven rear wheels are affected, the car will be powered left or right on the straight as the oversize tyre drives its side further per revolution than the nominal-size tyre. This is known as 'stagger' and in USAC-style paved track racing where the cars only turn left anyway, stagger may actually be built-in to a chassis. In this case the right rear wheel carries an oversize tyre, and the car's whole suspension system is set-up to bias it into a left-hand turn. The driver may have to apply slight right-hand steering lock to aim his car along the short straights, and the car will then enter the left-hand turns under power, finding its own stability.

All we need now is the engine, chassis, front suspension, fuel tanks and driver. Modern Formula 1 cars using the engine as a stressed chassis component break down into a series of individual sections. One of the easiest to move around is the rear suspension, normally mounted on the gearbox as in this case. Coil-springs wrapped round their adjustable dampers are visible, as is the curved anti-roll bar on top and the cooling vents in the brake discs mounted inboard against the gearbox cheeks.

The force which loads the tyre on to the road surface is known as the wheel loading and this is a function of the vehicle's gross weight and of its weight distribution. After a period of experimentation with extreme rearward weight distributions, a modern Formula 1 car has about 40 per cent of its weight supported on its front wheels and 60 per cent on the rear, when weighed on a weighbridge.

In action, the picture differs from moment to split-second moment as the car accelerates, squatting extra load down on to its rear wheels, or as it brakes – diving extra load forward on to its front wheels. When it rolls in corners the outside tyres are loaded-up while the inside tyres are lightly-laden and – if the suspension is strongly resistant to roll – they may even be plucked from the road surface leaving the car to corner on two or three wheels.

This effect may be minimised and influenced by the addition of aerodynamic aids such as aerofoil wing sections on the car's nose and tail. In sports cars with fully-enveloping bodyshells, extreme aerodynamic forces are harnessed by the much greater bodyshell area on which the airstream may react. Racing car aerodynamics is a science still to be completely understood and minor tweaks can transform a car's performance in seconds from fantastic to awful.

A car's suspension is not merely designed to unite wheel and chassis with a fair chance they never part company. Any lever arm rotating around a given point is said to have a certain 'geometry'; that is, its extremity describes a given arc as it moves up and down. With modern wide-tread racing tyres, the Formula 1 suspension system must control that arc as the road wheel bumps and droops over irregular road surfaces. It must limit the degree to which the wheel leans out or in at its extremes of movement, for these 'camber changes' may up-edge the tyre and reduce drastically – and dramatically – its contact area with the road. Should this happen grip would be lost abruptly and with it would go the driver's control.

Suspension geometry inevitably produces an imaginary point – the 'roll centre' – about which the car will roll when it corners and as centrifugal force reacts the chassis against its springs, suspension arms and ultimately the grip of those hard-pressed tyres.

How much a car rolls is dependent upon the centrifugal force to which its driver is subjecting it; the distance between the level of its centre of gravity and that of its roll axis (an imaginary line drawn between its front and rear roll centres); the stiffness of its springs and anti-roll bars; and the effect of its suspension geometry.

A very low centre of gravity (with the mass of the car's structure, its engine, gearbox and fuel load all concentrated as close to the ground as possible) will minimise the changes of attitude created by cornering, accelerating and braking. This is purely because the forces involved may be considered as acting against the car's centre of gravity, and if that centre is very close to the car's contact patch at road level then there is a shorter lever to react against than if that centre is way up in the air.

With roll limited by a low 'C of G' the weight transfer side-to-side and end-to-end as the car corners, or is accelerated and braked, will be minimised and so wheel loadings will be maintained at a more constant level and the tyres will be enabled to work longer at their optimum efficiency.

If a car dives savagely under braking as its weight transfers forward, its lightly laden rear tyres will lose efficiency and will easily lock, so contributing nothing (since they have 'broken away') to the slowing of the car.

However, under acceleration, pronounced rearward weight transference might be advantageous, since it would enhance traction from the driven tyres. But then steering, with the front wheels very lightly laden, would be vague to say the least, and this conditioned 'power under-steer' can be just as unpleasant as that of poor rear-end traction is frustrating.

Weight distributions may be shuffled about by the careful distribution of hefty components about the car. Once upon a time, a Grand Prix or sports-racing car would be designed and built then tested until its drivers pronounced themselves satisfied with its 'handling'. The team would then go racing, and apart from the fitting of fresh engines, gearboxes and tyres, and topping up with fuel and fluids, the car would remain unchanged thereafter. In the early 1960s the adjustable racing car began to appear, with teams

A study in balance: Niki Lauda in his Ferrari at Monaco. The cantilever effect of front and rear wings is obvious, while ducts feed air into the front wheels to cool the disc brakes mounted there, and body ducts feed air around the cockpit into the mid-engine, away from the radiators behind the front suspension, and into the oil coolers ahead of the rear wheels.

adopting differing stiffnesses of anti-roll bar and road springs from circuit to circuit. Today, this adjustability has assumed immense proportions, for not only are springs and roll-bars tailored from circuit to circuit, but suspension track widths and wheelbase lengths may be altered several times during practice and the race itself, all within a single meeting. In addition, engine and gearbox may be moved further apart or mounted closer together to effect weight distribution changes, and items like oil and water radiators often migrate in search of an optimum car balance front to rear. Add the fine tweaks possible with aerodynamic adjustment and you have a problem with so many variables that even top team engineers occasionally clap hands to head and exclaim, 'It's no good. We've chased ourselves up a tree. Let's go back to square one and start again!'

In 1976 a minor relocation of James Hunt's McLaren M23 oil

coolers made all the difference in making that car sufficiently competitive to steal the World Championship in the last half of the season; and in 1977 a similar change, with twin midship oil coolers replaced by a single cooler in the nosecone, made his later McLaren M26 a winning proposition.

The McLarens have all been long wheelbase cars with wide tracks, front and rear, with all the accepted characteristics such features give a car like making it relatively docile, stable, and easy to drive – though slow to change direction when a tight Ess-bend demands it.

Cars like Niki Lauda's Ferraris or the Tyrrells with which Jackie Stewart won his second two World Championships, have had shorter wheelbases which make them nervous and twitchy to handle, but exceptionally fast in the hands of an extremely skilful and sensitive driver. When Stewart retired at the end of 1973 and his experienced team-mate François Cevert was killed, Tyrrell designer Derek Gardner had to produce new cars for two relative newcomers in Jody Scheckter and Patrick Depailler, and he went for a longer wheelbase car which would be more stable, more forgiving and easier to drive though a little restricted in its outright performance potential.

Such theory and practice is at its most-developed level in Formula 1 racing, but the basic characteristics are alike in whatever class one cares to consider. Although there is only one Grands Prix race in each country every year (apart from the vast expanse of the USA which can absorb both East and West Coast Grands Prix without flooding its market) there are races for, say, Formula Ford cars all over the world almost every weekend.

Any good racing car manufacturer produces some kind of specification sheet for the cars he builds, and the owners campaigning his product will only excel if they begin their own development at the point for which their car was designed. Basic settings like ride heights, castors, cambers, toe-ins (the plan-view settings of the wheels), spring rates, damper types, recommended brake pads and suggested make of tyre and their ideal rolling diameters should all be known.

Lola Cars of Huntingdon, England, are the world's biggest

racing car manufacturers and their specification folders on their cars include such basic setting-up instructions as the following – actually on a T330 F5000 model:

'Front suspension:	Castor	$3\frac{1}{2}$ degrees
	Camber	Zero
	Wheel alignment	From zero to 1/16 inch total tow-in
	Dampers	5 clicks on from the off position'

This 'instruction manual' then proceeds to explain how adjustments should be made only after the static ride height has been fixed by disconnecting the spring/damper units, chocking the chassis on a 3-inch block at the front and a $3\frac{1}{2}$-inch block at the rear, then adjusting the screw-thread tuning arrangements built-in to the suspension members.

I once did a lot of work with the veteran Australian racing driver Frank Gardner, who was Lola's development pilot as well as British Champion Driver and who made a splendid career out of driving everything from big American saloon cars to Formula 1 and 7-litre Ford GTs at Le Mans.

Frank explained the setting-up of typical minor-Formula single-seaters and since this is what is going on during practice sessions at race circuits all over the world, it is worth repeating for the interest of the racing spectator.

One prerequisite for the competitor is to ensure that all his tyres have the same rolling diameter, for discrepancies in manufacture have been known and odd-sized tyres can affect handling quite dramatically.

With the car set-up as the manufacturer suggests, the first task is to establish a comfortable lap-time around whatever circuit it may be – perhaps Brands Hatch for the sake of argument. This will be the lap speed which the driver feels secure and confident producing; a time he could repeat all day long if necessary. By sticking his neck out he may be able to equal his – or the car's previous owner's – best Brands Hatch time, but now is the time for fine tuning.

Most rear-engined (or more properly, 'mid-engined') racing cars have a degree of rake built into them – that is they sit on the road slightly nose-down. Front ride height may be around $3\frac{1}{2}$ inches, with rear ride height around 4 inches. This kind of rake, coupled to sensible anti-roll bars should balance the car quite nicely, make it receptive to aerodynamic effects, and responsive to drive. Should the driver find his car's front-end washing out into a chronic understeer – with its front wheels losing adhesion before the rears – a first move to combat the effect is to lower the front a little. This increases forward weight transfer, loads-up the front tyres and improves their grip. This is done in the more sophisticated Formulae by adjusting the dampers and their threaded coil-spring platforms to drop the chassis. In simple Formulae,

The experimental six-wheeled ELF Tyrrell P34 was a design exercise by Derek Gardner (*right*) for Ken Tyrrell (*left*) which very nearly achieved major success before tyre development problems killed it. Patrick Depailler is in the cockpit, and the French ELF oil company which sponsored the car found it magnificent publicity.

where adjustable dampers are far too expensive, a minor machining job may be necessary to shorten the dampers themselves.

However, before anything so drastic is attempted, the driver must ensure his car is not hitting its bump stops under braking. Ideally the suspension should meet its stops just before the underside of the nosecone brushes the road surface. If the car rests on its stops before nearing the road then a stiffer spring is required to lift it. To cure that understeer a softer anti-roll bar, less likely to lift the inside wheel clear of the road while cornering, would help. If stiffer springs are fitted and the bottoming is cured, then a too-stiff anti-roll bar will reveal itself by lifting the inside wheel while cornering.

In these conditions, the car will not be at all responsive and the driver will be gaining little 'feel' through his steering wheel. Now with stiffer springs the front end can be lowered once more and this time the weight transference should be nicely controlled and a few more laps will tell the driver if he has gone too hard with those springs.

Too hard and the car will behave as badly as when it was bottoming. Its wheels will not follow the road surface as faithfully as they should and the car will be twitchy and uncontrollable. If the uprated springs work well and the front ride height adjustment leaves the ride acceptable there may still be a touch too much understeer remaining. Now, recommended Frank, is the time to try a different anti-roll bar. Effectively, the less roll resistance the better the grip, and so an anti-roll bar of less resistance will be fitted – perhaps a bar of thinner metal, or a tubular bar which has been drilled.

If this work does not tame the car and produce a good-riding, predictable set-up which follows the road surface nicely it is time for the driver to suspect the understeer is caused by too much roll at the rear end.

In this case, harder rear springs are fitted, and if this kills the understeer and replaces it with a mild oversteer characteristic then the driver concerned may accept it as it stands or perhaps soften-up the rear anti-roll bar to balance front and rear-end grip more closely.

Still Frank – as a very experienced racing driver – was very conscious that road conditions may change drastically during the course of a race, and emphasised the importance of a chassis being set-up in a versatile manner. When oil is laid down a car with stiff suspension and anti-roll bars will not give its driver the feel and sensitivity he needs. Softer bars allow better feel and in a class like radial-tyred Formula Ford this is especially important.

There is a definite limit to how hard springs can go, for every spring compression is followed by its rebound and the car's dampers have to be man enough to absorb that rebound and control it properly. If rebound control is lacking then the car concerned will leap and bound from bump to bump, will lock wheels and lose

Some glorious circuits survive, such as the Österreichring in Austria where Grand Prix cars howl around the Styrian countryside.

adhesion under braking. It will lose time and be a certain candidate for an accident.

Castor adjustment governs the self-centring action and kick-back of the steering and it may be wound-off until the car is no longer stable in a straight line. Ideally, enough castor should be adopted to have the car running straight while the steering remains as light and with as little tiring kick-back as possible.

For very fast circuits, there are special tweaks to be used even in the most humble Formulae, such as ensuring that the wheel bearings are not screwed-up too tight, and possibly filing the brake pads a little to ensure they sit loose around the disc and so minimise the car's mechanical drag. On the 'non-wing Formulae' cars there is little to be done aerodynamically when a very fast circuit is encountered, except to ensure the car rakes down at the front – and to tape over any yawning bodywork joints or cracks which may add a little aerodynamic drag.

When cars are raced with wings at front and rear drivers, designers and engineers strive to balance the set of purchases which is involved front to rear. If the front wings produce 100 lb of downthrust then the rear wing must produce a commensurate amount to maintain a balance in the car. It is possible to adjust a rear wing to produce so much downforce that the car will lift its nose at speed and will wash out into an instant understeer when the driver attempts to head it into a corner. Similarly, a car with too much downforce on the front will always be looking early into corners, it will be unstable on the straight, very twitchy, prone to lurid oversteer and utterly diabolical under braking as its rear wheels run light and lock-up. It is relatively easy for an inexperienced team or driver to put themselves into such a situation and then fail to recognise it as an aerodynamic maladjustment and to work furiously on the suspension.

Neither is it possible to set a car to its aerodynamic optimum in private testing, for the turbulent slipstream conditions of racing in traffic can cause great trouble. If a car is marginally nose-heavy aerodynamically, then the moment its driver dodges out of the slipstream from a car ahead and encounters clean air he will find his mount ducked down, suddenly weaving and tail-happy. This may be more confidence destroying than actually dangerous, but confidence is a vital contribution to a racing driver's success or failure. Conversely, if the car is trimmed slightly tail-heavy then the instant it emerges from a slipstream to encounter clean air its nose will begin to lift and the steering will assume a very eerie lightness . . . On a fast and smooth circuit it may be possible to camouflage the effects of poor aerodynamic adjustment by fitting harder rear springs to stop the tail sagging, which will produce intractable and twitchy handling. If they try the same ploy on the front the car will prove too stiff and rigid to follow the road surface faithfully, and spectators will see those characteristic puffs of blue smoke as front wheels lock and tyres burn. While this set-up may brake well on the smooth expanse of Silverstone, it would prove virtually undriveable over the bumps and dips at Brands Hatch.

With the car set-up by team and driver to suit local conditions, with all these myriad combinations dialled-in to form an efficient compromise, the motor race is ready to begin – and from this point on, the racing driver is alone.

3 Driving as an Art

Race driving is not a simple matter of starting your car, smashing your throttle foot to the floor and holding it there for the duration. Dependent upon the rewards awaiting the result, the type of competition and the class of race, top-level success is often a case of surviving to the finish flag at the lowest – rather than the highest – possible speed. The old truism in motor racing is: 'To finish first you must first finish' – and Fangio (who was fond of that saying) was not the first to believe that it was logical to proceed as slowly as the opposition will let you.

'Slowly' is of course a relative term and there is a long-established system of rating a driver's effort by a system of tenths. Driving at seven-tenths of maximum effort might be a reliable, intelligent approach to an endurance race, while trying harder at eight-tenths might be the level at which a Grand Prix driver races home towards the end of a gruelling race. Nine-tenths driving will be very near the limit, used by clubmen in short-distance events or by the aces in a fairly fierce and valuable dice. Ten-tenths driving is rarely seen except when an exceptionally important prize is at stake, and driving at eleven-tenths is seen more often as driver error attempts the impossible and an accident ensues! It is also very true that what is seven-tenths driving for an ace may be eleven-tenths for an also-ran, and there are numerous examples of drivers clambering shamefacedly from a pile of smoking wreckage after trying to follow a Fangio, Moss or Stewart at *their* pace . . .

Racing drivers come in all shapes and sizes, and the flaxen-haired James Hunt hero type are few and far between. Good eyes, brisk minds and a restless desire 'to be better' are common, and

Golden Boy: Stirling Moss – indisputably the greatest post-war racing driver never to become World Champion; in itself this is a condemnation of the Championship system.

with very few exceptions top drivers have remarkably bright and penetrating eyes with remarkable depth perception and resolution. Today's drivers recline in machines which subject their bodies to quite savage forces, and highly-developed shoulder and neck muscles develop to support heavy-helmeted heads against 1·4 (or more) times the force of gravity in corners.

Great drivers – those who set the performance standards of their time – are few and far between. Since World War II, those who have led the way in major-league road racing are Jean-Pierre Wimille, Juan-Manuel Fangio, Stirling Moss, Jimmy Clark and Jackie Stewart. Niki Lauda has proved himself as the most intelligent driver of current times, but a general levelling-out of achievement makes the title of 'standard-setter' seem arguable with drivers like James Hunt, Jody Scheckter, Mario Andretti and perhaps Ronnie Peterson all somewhere in the pecking order.

Juan Manuel Fangio, in Alfa Corse's supercharged straight-8 $1\frac{1}{2}$-litre Alfetta at Silverstone during the 1951 British GP where these cars were beaten for the first time by Gonzalez's $4\frac{1}{2}$-litre unsupercharged V12 Ferrari.

To a certain extent, the popular media impression of the 'fearless young man' type of driver may be true. Some certainly have no conception of personal danger, but this type seldom fulfils the basic rule and survives to the finish of a race. Others may be physically sick from pre-race tension, yet as soon as they are strapped into their cars and the flag drops they may perform like supermen. For most of his time on circuit the great racing driver will be working way out in the border country of his own ability, and with his pursuers to force him on there can be little held in reserve. It is the capacity of effort in reserve which makes a good racing driver into a great one – the old business of one man's nine-tenths effort being another man's ten-tenths once again.

Three World Champions in a memorable race: Jack Brabham leads Jim Clark and Denny Hulme in the 1966 Dutch GP where Jimmy's 2-litre Lotus stayed with the 3-litre Brabhams for much of the distance.

A lay person's reaction to being driven in a competition car by any experienced racing driver might be that they could never do that, they would not be brave enough to enter corners with so little in reserve. In comparison, the performance of the true ace is on an almost unreal level. It might be a case of thinking 'Even if I was brave enough, there is no way that I could make a car do that!' While the run-of-the-mill driver would be chancing his arm on every corner, operating a nano-second – a thousandth millionth of one second – behind the reactions of his car to catch its every slide and twitch, the genuine ace operates ahead of his conveyance. He has the sensitivity and skill to take that vehicle by the scruff of its neck and can actually make it slide, corner, break traction and make traction as his natural instincts tell him the situation requires. Nuvolari explained to his protégé Giuseppe Farina in the 1930s: 'Your car must be a living thing – never for one moment must you let it hang dead . . .' and today, an age away from Nuvolari's kind of racing, that still holds true.

The great racing driver will be striving to funnel every motion of his car into the unattainable perfect lap, and success settles on the fastest attainable time on every race lap. Add the complication of competition and back-marker traffic to be passed during a race, and the primary aim becomes one merely of staying in front with quick lap times as a by-product. In this way, motor racing becomes a truly combative activity in which the stakes are high,

Unexpected hazard: Österreichring wildlife as a deer decides to cross the circuit in front of a practising Formula 1 car.

and the make-up of the racing driver mind makes him unlikely to settle willingly for second best.

There is an element of luck in the natural attributes which make a great racing driver great. He does not require the finely honed musculature of a top-flight athlete but he must be fit; far fitter than the general public might imagine for the heat and continuous G-force sustained in a really fast car's cockpit drains pounds of weight, vital fluid, salt and reserves of energy during a long, hard race.

The driver's perceptive abilities must be exceptional. Keen eyes and supremely sensitive balance organs must feed the brain with stimuli upon which it reacts with nano-second reflex. Sinew and muscle must respond with finely-judged and natural reactions which balance the car on its slippery knife-edge between optimum performance and loss of control.

These basic abilities must be inborn while time spent in the extraordinary environment of a racing car at speed may in time produce experienced reaction and conditioned reflex which combine to form control. Experience and, above all, a steely determination to succeed has made winners out of drivers who had relatively little going for them naturally. These drivers have in some cases become World Champions – men like Graham Hill and Denny Hulme for example – but they never made it as standard-setters of their time. They were never equal blow-for-blow with Fangio, Moss, Clark or Stewart.

Above all, nobody will get to the top in such a fiercely competitive endeavour without the determination and dedication to carve themselves a place. Many drivers (and journalists) receive thousands of letters every month, and a large proportion will be from not-so-youthful admirers saying 'I want to be a racing driver, how do I start?' With few exceptions theirs is a hopeless cause, for if they were going to succeed they would have found their way into a motor club and would have started already, without help.

In recent years an extra aspect of sensitivity has become as important as the ability to drive quickly and intelligently in a race. As the racing car has become increasingly adjustable, so the man who can most effectively test, adjust and develop his car to match the latest set of requirements is the man who will lead the way. The man who can combine such technical ability with sheer speed in qualifying and intelligent pace in the race will – with good fortune on his side – be the man who wins.

On Circuit

In a modern Grand Prix race, where 26 cars' practice times may be spread over as little as 0·96 seconds, a front-row of the grid starting position is of enormous assistance. When cars are that evenly matched it is an advantage to start with clear road ahead, and the name of the game then will be to maintain that position and keep the pack behind. The same is true to a certain extent in short-distance club races where there is often insufficient time in the eight to ten laps duration to fight back into the lead after an early setback, or a starting position far down the starting grid.

Grid positions were at one time decided by ballot, but for many years now the more just system has been adopted of deciding grid positions on the basis of practice lap times. For a major race, at least two timed practice periods and a third, untimed, 'setting-up' session may be scheduled while, for a minor club event, practice may simply be a brief 20-minute blast on race morning. In either event, the period is used to acclimatise the driver to the circuit conditions (or to its layout if he has never been there before), and to set-up the car to achieve its optimum performance at this venue. Obviously it is very difficult to tune a club car perfectly in the brief practice period available, particularly when the driver must set a competitive time if he is not to be buried near the back of the starting grid.

It is always interesting for the enthusiastic race spectator to arrive early and watch what goes on in these sessions. If a driver has new tyres and brake pads fitted (as he most certainly will if this is an international event) he will be seen spending his first exploratory laps bedding them in, assessing the circuit, and judging how well his chosen gear ratios match the course. Unlike a road car gearbox, most racing transmissions offer easy interchangeability of gear ratios. Thus, for a tight and twisty course, low gear ratios will be adopted, allowing the engine to achieve its peak power within the short straights available to it. Running such a low-geared car on a faster course would be hopeless for its engine would be over-revving wildly long before the cut-off point on a long straight, and the more highly geared competition would draw away; their engines running more slowly at far higher road speeds. Undergearing for a circuit provides punch out of slow corners, but can never be competitive. Slight over-gearing can always be made competitive and is important at club level where the engine and gearbox is given an easier time, and its expensive life is lengthened!

French power: the Matra V12 engine was designed for Formula 1 and sports car racing in 1968, came to dominate the endurance class and Le Mans but into 1978 had won only twice in Grand Prix cars.

Any engine has a 'torque band' between certain revolution speeds at which it produces most punch. Drivers will gear their cars to fall back into the meat of this torque band as they change up, and engine revs fall back before accelerating once more. In recent years, in Formula I racing, it has become necessary to offer the driver six gear ratios instead of five to keep his high-revving engine within its narrow torque band most of the time.

Gearing a little on the high side enables the driver to use another car's slipstream with impunity on a fast circuit, as this suction effect will tow him along at higher speeds than he could achieve solo. Gearing a little on the high side also helps eliminate gear changing, and that eliminates one more chance of missing a change and damaging the engine by over-revving it. It is also one less change to load the clutch and gearbox internals which have a limited working life in any case.

After his exploratory laps, the driver will find his car properly

Modern racing tyres are broad and bald in order to place the maximum possible area of rubber in contact with the road. The three diagonal slots allow tread depth to be measured.

warmed-up, the drag from cold engine and gearbox oil will be minimised as it has heated-up, and tyres and brake pads will be approaching their peak-efficiency temperatures. A thoughtless driver can ruin his car's braking by using it too fiercely before the pads are warm. The sudden heating of the pad surface pulls the copper impregnation out of the pad and welds it to the disc surface. When this 'de-naturing' process occurs, the uneven disc surface will knock-back the pads when they are applied in braking and the pedal will feel soft and retardation will be poor. Drivers bed in tyres and brakes very carefully before fading-out the brake pads often in one savage and spectacular stamp from near top speed. After this gentle bedding-in, followed by savage overheating, the pads are race-ready. Brand-new tyres offer very little grip and even brainless Grand Prix drivers have had enormous accidents through pressing too hard, too soon, on cold and new tyres. They have to be scuffed-in and warmed to reach their optimum efficiency, and 'unscrubbed' tyres are notoriously like driving on ice. So the driver has a lot on his mind in these opening exploratory laps!

Every sensible competition car has an adjustable linkage behind its brake pedal which balances the braking effort fed to front and rear by the individual hydraulic master cylinders provided. Most drivers prefer a little extra braking effort on their front wheels. The car will tend to lock a front wheel under extreme load and a car which develops a little understeer in this way is always safe and predictable – in the dry. It is then always possible for the driver to ease off the pedal, unlock his front wheels, add steering lock and take another bite at the corner.

With the balance biased to the rear, however, a locking wheel will put the tail out, the car will look early into the corner and may well spin. With a rear wheel locked, any decent downshift through the gears will be difficult because the inertial powers which aid selection will have been killed. In any case, the overrun braking effect of the engine reacts through the rear wheels, and this will harass the balance of the car if the brakes themselves are biased to the rear. In wet weather, braking does tend to be rearward-biased, if only to decrease the likelihood of a front-end breakaway into a lurid locked-up understeer.

As practice reaches its climax, one may assume that every car is as well balanced and finely tuned as it is going to become, and at this time, usually well into the closing minutes, some heroic all-out driving will be seen to gain that possibly vital starting position. Fastest man overall gains the honour of pole position, which basically puts him on the inside line into the circuit's first corner – although in Formula 1 the pole position driver may be given the choice of which side of the track he prefers. The rest of the field will then follow suit, in today's Formula 1 racing being arranged two-by-two in descending lap time order, with the faster of each pair on the same side as the pole position.

Naturally, speed through corners is the key to competitive motor racing, for the less speed a car loses in a corner the higher speed it is likely to reach on the straight which follows. Exit speed from a corner determines maximum speed along the following straight and on some circuits, such as Zandvoort – venue for the annual Dutch Grand Prix – this may be all-important. There a medium-fast right-hander leads on to the long start–finish straight and cars slipstream one another for almost a mile down into a 180-degree hairpin known as the Tarzan Curve. This is virtually the only place on the circuit at which evenly matched cars may overtake, and the manoeuvre is made by entering the straight quickly enough to maintain close contact with the car ahead, then ducking out of its slipstream into the braking area at Tarzan, hopefully nipping off the leading car on the inside, forcing it wide and so going through on the shortest possible line.

'Line' is what high-speed driving and race driving is all about, for you will never see a racing field religiously following the kerb-lines of a circuit. They will sweep wide into corners, clip the inside apex of the turn on the way through and then run wide to the opposite kerb on the exit, accelerating hard and probably sliding slightly in the process.

The accepted art in cornering is to enter corners with the car slowed sufficiently to get round, and with it settled-down and stable. Then a combination of power and steering lock will balance the car through the turn on its racing 'line' and it should exit the turn like a bullet, accelerating hard all the way.

The two-by-two Grand Prix grid is standard practice today but at the time this photograph was taken – at Hockenheim for the 1970 German GP – it was fairly unusual, and unpopular, because the back row starters were already well over 100-metres down before the flag had dropped. On the front row here are Jochen Rindt's Lotus 72 and Jacky Ickx's Ferrari 312B.

Often spectators will see a car diving deep into a turn, then suddenly ducking as its driver smashes the brakes, and weaving wildly as he fights to control the inevitable suspension rebound to the action he has just induced. Top drivers are sensitive people when it comes to vehicle handling, and they will just brush in their brakes relatively lightly for what is actually only a fleeting instant, and only then with the car beginning to settle its rubber feet firmly into the road surface they bury the pedal hard. With the car sufficiently slowed, but *only* just sufficiently, the driver's right foot then dances back on to the throttle pedal and he toes the car out of the turn – the rear wheels providing the cornering power while the front wheels provide the balance through the driver's steering touch.

This business of using what is effectively 'the line of least resistance' through a corner is a natural thing; a pattern into which a smoothly fast-driven car will settle on its own if its driver is in rhythm with his machinery. After a few minutes at racing speeds, a race field will have laid down a trail of rubber impregnating the line through any corner, and off that line a layer of loose debris will await the unwary driver, off-line. Overtaking is usually achieved under braking into the corners rather than through them, and motor racing as a game of cut and thrust is seen at its best on the entry to the turns where fumble and out-fumble counts for everything.

Races are generally so short today that there is little room for master plans and team strategy except in the endurance classics which have survived, although their competition is so limited that it is more a matter of driving for a finish than of racing for a result. Still the intelligent racing driver will not smash his car over kerbs to save inches when tyre or suspension damage could cost him the race. Neither will he follow another car so closely that should the leading driver brake unduly early or perform some other unexpected manoeuvre the two cars will collide. The intelligent driver combines his own pace with the ability to stay out of trouble, and this all comes down to that old truism 'To finish first, you must first finish . . .'

Accidents do happen, and very often cars and drivers are put out of races by becoming involved in an incident which someone else's misjudgement or misfortune began. Lightning reflexes flurry into action in such instances, and more collisions have been avoided by ace drivers taking no avoiding action than by less capable hands dodging wildly, and losing control of their own cars. Fangio, Moss and Stewart all held that if you aimed for a spinning car, albeit while standing squarely on the brakes, the chances are that by the time you arrive it has spun away and the road will be clear. Nothing is guaranteed, but motor racing is that kind of game. The chances are carefully calculated, and often they come off.

Today, racing as a science and driving as an art are inextricably entwined. The age when a driver could report to his team engineer that the car '. . . is like a wild woman, it merely needs taming' are long gone, and the great racing driver's inbuilt sensitivity and skill is worth little if he has not got an understanding for the technicalities of his task. What goes on in a racing car cornering at its limits of adhesion and traction is an incredibly complex physics problem – and one which deep scientific investigation in recent years has yet satisfactorily to comprehend.

This lack of precise scientific understanding is what makes the driver's art as yet invaluable – since the great names of motor racing can instinctively comprehend effects which are still scientifically incalculable . . .

As I wrote in the beginning, there is more to race driving than meets the eye.

4 The Major Championships

Obviously the International Championship series which attracts most public interest is the World Drivers' competition decided by the national Grand Prix races of each season, but there are many other less well-publicised Championships which are also of international significance. These competitions are arranged as follows:

World Championship of Drivers

Decided on a points basis between drivers of Formula 1 cars contesting the World Championship Grand Prix race series.

Qualifying Grand Prix races must not exceed a length of 200 miles or duration of two hours, and must not cover less than 250 km (155·376 miles). If the entire distance has not been completed by the two-hour time limit, the chequered flag will be shown to the leader of the race at the end of the lap during which two hours was exceeded.

Qualifying events (1978) were arranged as follows:

Part One:

Argentine GP	Buenos Aires
Brazilian GP	Rio de Janeiro
South African GP	Kyalami
US GP West	Long Beach
Monaco GP	Monte Carlo
Belgian GP	Zolder
Spanish GP	Jarama

Part Two:

Swedish GP	Anderstorp
French GP	Ricard-Castellet
British GP	Brands Hatch
German GP	Hockenheim
Austrian GP	Osterreichring
Dutch GP	Zandvoort
Italian GP	Monza
US GP East	Watkins Glen
Canadian GP	Mosport Park

Championship points are awarded on the following scale:

1st place	9 points
2nd place	6 points
3rd place	4 points
4th place	3 points
5th place	2 points
6th place	1 point

Points are only awarded if the driver has driven the same car throughout the qualifying event, i.e. drivers who have changed cars are ineligible for points. There is a limitation on the number of points which may be counted towards a driver's end of season total, in that the championship season is divided into two halves – or when the number of events actually run is uneven, into two sections with one more race in the early-season section than in the later one. A driver may only count a number of point scores equal to the number of events in each section, less one. This, in effect, means that he will drop only his worst points score if he has been lucky enough to finish in the first six in every race of that section, which is a rare occurrence. In practice drivers are normally in a position at the end of the year to count every point they have scored.

World Championship race organisers are free to admit Formula 2 cars and drivers if the number of Formula 1 cars available is insufficient. Both Formula 2 cars (running without weight handicap) and their drivers will be eligible for the World

Championships, and Formula 2 car entrants must share the recognised Formula 1 financial provisions (i.e. – an organiser cannot fill his grid with 'cheap' Formula 2 cars, and the Formula 2 entrants must accept the prize money share-out organised by the Formula 1 Constructors' Association).

International Cup for Formula 1 Constructors

This 'Constructors' Championship' goes to the most successful chassis constructor in the Championship-qualifying Grand Prix series, and on two occasions – in 1958 and 1973 – the winning team was not that of the World Champion driver. Mike Hawthorn won the Drivers' title in Ferrari cars in the former season although Vanwall amassed more Constructors' Championship points, while in the latter season, Jackie Stewart was Champion Driver in his Tyrrell cars yet Lotus (under their John Player Special name) won the Constructors' title.

Points are awarded on the same basis as the Drivers' Championship, but naturally go to the chassis manufacturer rather than to the driver himself (or herself).

One significant difference is that a constructor is only permitted to count one points-scoring finish in each race, therefore if he entered two cars, one finished first and the other second – then only the winner's nine points would be added to the constructor's Championship total. The six points for second place would be withheld, and the third place car would then take its normal four points for its constructor. In this way a team which happened to have a brainstorm, enters say five cars for one race, and is lucky enough to have them finish 1–2–3–4–5, would not accumulate such a massive points total as to put it beyond reach of its less well-endowed competitors.

World Championship for Makes

Descendant of the old Sports Car World Championship, this competition is open to vehicles from Groups 1 to 5, with two divisions – up to 2 litres, and over 2 litres engine capacity. These Groups are recognised as follows:

- Group 1 Series-Production Touring Cars (5,000-off in 12 months)
- Group 2 Touring Cars (1,000-off in 12 months)
- Group 3 Series-Production GT Cars (at least 2 seats, 1,000-off)
- Group 4 Grand Touring Cars (at least 2 seats, 400-off in 24 months)
- Group 5 Special Production Cars (derived from the above groups with no minimum production requirement)

Sports cars storm into the first turn at Nürburgring at the start of the 1970 ADAC 1,000-kilometre race. For complex reasons sports car racing virtually died as the 1970s progressed. Leading here are the Porsche 908/3s of Rodriguez and Jo Siffert – both quite outstanding drivers in this type of car.

World Championship of Makes qualifying races have to be of 6-Hours to 12-Hours in duration unless they have been established traditionally at some other standard, such as the Nurburgring 1,000-km race. Replacement at the pits of such major items as engine block, cylinder head, gearbox and differential casings are

Nürburgring, Germany.

forbidden, oil levels may only be replenished beyond 220-km intervals, only four mechanics are allowed to work on a car in the pits at any one time, and up to three drivers may be named for each car; they may also share a second entry.

Qualifying events (1978) included:

Daytona 24-hours	USA
Mugello	Italy
Dijon 1,000 km	France
Spa Grand Prix	Belgium
Silverstone 6-hours	Great Britain
Nürburgring 1,000 km	Germany
Osterreichring	Austria
Watkins Glen 6-hours	USA
Mosport	Canada
Vallelunga	Italy
Estoril	Portugal
Hockenheim	Germany

Sadly, vehicles eligible for this Championship are extremely expensive to acquire and run, and without Porsche's active support the series would almost certainly die. As it is, several qualifying rounds are cancelled each year due to lack of support and spectator interest. Championship points are awarded on the following scales:

1st place	20 points
2nd place	15 points
3rd place	12 points
4th place	10 points
5th place	8 points
6th place	6 points
7th place	5 points
8th place	3 points
9th place	2 points
10th place	1 point

Point scores retained at the end of the Championship will be decided on the number of events actually organised, as follows:

From 6 events actually organised, scores retained will be total, less one.
From 7 to 9 events, scores retained will be total, less two.
From 10 to 12 events, scores retained will be total, less three.
From more than 12 events, scores retained will be total, less four.

If less than two-thirds the number of qualifying events scheduled in the international calendar should take place, then the Championship will be considered void. Points are awarded in each capacity division and the highest aggregate total at the end of the series, from whichever division, is declared Champion.

European Championship for Sports Cars

After the failure of a so-called 'World Championship' for this class of car in 1977, when entries were hopelessly thin, the competition was confined to European status for 1978. Eligible cars were from Groups 5 (qv) and 6 – the latter effectively being classical-style open cockpit two-seat sports-racing cars – arranged in two categories; one for special racing engines of 3-litres (normally aspirated) or 2·14 litres supercharged and 5-litre production block engines – the second for 2-litre normally-aspirated engines, or supercharged engines of a capacity decided by a 1·4 division factor (i.e. 2,000 cc ÷ 1·4 = 1,428 cc). Duration of qualifying events to be two hours or 250 km minimum or not more than four hours' maximum. Established traditional distance events are exempt. Points are awarded on the Championship of Makes basis, to the successful drivers. The driver with the highest aggregate total at the completion of the season is declared Champion.

Qualifying events (1978) included:

Goodyear '200'	Nürburgring, Germany
Monza 1,000 km	Italy
Vallelunga	Italy
Imola	Italy
Estoril	Portugal
Vacations Trophy	Jarama, Spain
Coppa Florio	Enna, Sicily

Interest centred upon the Italian Alfa Romeo team, the only works organisation to support the whole series, hence the strong Italian race bias.

European Championship for Formula 2 Drivers

Of far more significance, the European Formula 2 Championship as it is known is the training ground from which many Formula 1 drivers have graduated. Formula 2 regulations demand single-seater racing cars with unsupercharged engines of not more than 2 litres capacity, and weighing not less than 500 kg (1,102 lb). Engines may be of free design (i.e. not based on production units) but must have no more than six cylinders. No more than five forward gears are permitted in the gearbox and no more than two wheels may be powered (thus four-wheel drive is banned). Bodywork overhangs (measured from the front and rear axles) must not exceed 100 cm at the front and 80 cm at the rear, while maximum overall width is limited to 200 cm. Overall maximum width of the rear wheels (hence available tyre size) is limited to 16 inches, while their diameter is compulsory at 13 inches.

Cars eligible for the European Championship are only of Formula 2 type, and no other.

Qualifying events may be run in two or more qualifying heats and a final, or in two equal heats producing an aggregate result, or as a single race only.

Maximum distance for one heat is 175 km (108·763 miles).

Maximum total distance for an event including more than one heat is 325 km (201·988 miles).

Maximum total distance for a single race is 225 km (139·838 miles).

Driver Eligibility

A system has recently been introduced whereby the FIA recognises what it calls A, B and C category driver licences. A C-licence is the most humble international level which indicates the driver has satisfactorily completed a certain number of minor home events in the organisers' view and is therefore considered suitably qualified to 'go international'.

To qualify for a B-licence, necessary to compete in Formula 2, Formula 5,000, Groups 5 and 6 and International Formula Atlantic, the C-licence driver must have finished in the first five in five representative level races within the preceding twelve-month period.

Then to qualify for an A-licence, which will allow the driver to compete in Formula 1 and USAC Championship events, the driver must achieve similar results within Category B races within a previous twelve-month period, except in the case of Formula Atlantic events in which a total of ten first-five results must have been obtained within a twenty-four-month period. All classifications must have been obtained in National Championship or

International Championship circuit events. The driver who holds a superior category licence is qualified for lesser categories of car.

This system is of vital significance in the European Formula 2 Championship in which only drivers not qualified for Grand Prix competition are eligible for points.

Points are awarded on a Formula 1 standard, with Championship of Makes-style score selection towards the end of season total.

European Championship for Formula 3 Drivers

Another step down the ladder, in which drivers of Formula 3 cars only will be eligible.

International Formula 3 demands single-seater racing cars using not more than four-cylinder, production-based engines of up to 2 litres capacity. The basic engine must be of a type of which at least 5,000 units have been manufactured within twelve consecutive months and modifications are strictly regulated. The engine's induction system is free apart from a ban on supercharging (i.e. the use of either carburettors or fuel injection is permitted) but the system must draw its air through a 'throttling flange' 3 mm in thickness and not more than 24 mm in diameter. This limitation on the air entering the unit places an effective ceiling on the power it will produce.

Dimensional limitations include a minimum wheelbase of 200 cm (to outlaw 'kart-type' vehicles), a minimum track width of 120 cm and a maximum wheel rim width of 10 inches. Front and rear overhangs, measured from the axles, are 100 cm front and 80 cm rear while overall width is limited to 185 cm.

Tyre restrictions are applied in that tread width must not exceed 8 inches on compulsory 13-inch diameter wheels.

Minimum weight, without ballast, is 440 kg.

Championship-qualifying events may be run in various eliminating heats not exceeding 50 km and a final of 100 km, or in two 75-km heats. Overall race distance must not exceed 150 km. Drivers score points on a World Drivers' Championship basis.

European Hill-Climb Championship

At one time a very significant series in which the might of the Mercedes-Benz, Auto Union, Alfa Romeo and later Ferrari and Porsche factory teams became involved, the European Hill-Climb Championship has declined in recent years. It is essentially another Driver's Championship, open to Groups 1–4 cars in a Category A and to Groups 5–6 cars in Category B. Various minor capacity subdivisions are provided and four-wheel drive is forbidden.

Qualifying hill-climb courses are all much longer than, say, those in Great Britain. Requirements include a minimum distance of 5 km; a minimum change in level from start to finish of 350 m; a minimum average upward gradient of 5 per cent, and there must be no more than one-fifth of the entire distance where this gradient averages less than 2 per cent. Each competitor must

Serious hill-climbing, 1904 style, as Vincenzo Lancia charges up the Susa-Monte Cenisio mountain course to win in his 75 hp FIAT.

cover a minimum distance of 10 km during his qualifying runs, and electrical timing accurate to at least one-hundredth of a second shall be used. Points are awarded on the normal driver basis, only to those who completed their climbs within 120 per cent of the fastest time in their class, and at the end of the series only drivers who scored in at least one-third of the events actually organised will be eligible. The highest aggregate points total in Category A gives the successful driver the title of – and only the French could think of it – 'European Hill-Climb for Production Cars Champion' – or in Category B 'European Hill-Climb for Competition Cars Champion'.

Qualifying events (1978) included:

Ampus-Draguignan	France
Col St Pierre	France
Alpl	Austria
Serra da Estrela	Portugal
Montseny	Spain
Freiburg-Schauinsland	Germany
Coppa Sila	Italy
Trento Bondone	Italy
Dobratsch	Austria
Chamrousse	France
Coppa Carotti	Italy
Mont Dore	France
St Ursanne les Rangiers	Switzerland
Los Montes de Malaga	Spain
Cefalu Gibilmanna	Italy

European Championship for Touring Cars

This competition reserves two titles, one for the victorious marque; the other for the most successful driver. It is open to Group 2 cars divided into the following classes: from 1,000 to 1,300 cc; over 1,300 cc to 1,600 cc; over 1,600 cc to 2,000 cc; over 2,000 cc to 3,000 cc; and above, 3,000 cc.

Qualifying events are all circuit races which must last at least 3½ hours or cover a minimum of 500 km (312 miles) – remember the classic Grand Prix distance?

Two drivers must share the driving of each car. Both marques and drivers will be awarded Championship points on a Championship of Makes (first ten places qualify) scale. A marque will be declared Champion only if it has accumulated 70 points or more in the series. A driver must have covered one-third total race distance to qualify for points, and if he has driven more than one car he shall be ineligible for points. The highest-scoring driver at the end of the season is awarded the European Cup for Touring Cars.

Qualifying events (1978) were arranged as follows:

Brands Hatch	Great Britain
Monza	Italy
Salzburgring	Austria
Mugello	Italy
Jarama	Spain
Estoril	Portugal
Österreichring	Austria
Brno	Czechoslovakia
Nürburgring	Germany
Zandvoort	Netherlands
Silverstone	Great Britain
Zolder	Belgium
Ricard-Castellet	France

The Other Championships

Apart from these more major competitions, which in fact attract very variable support from the heights of Formula 1 to the obscurity of the European Sports and Hill-Climb Championships, the FIA also sanctions a World and European Rally Championship (which is beyond the scope of this book), a European Rallycross Cup for Drivers, and a European Cup for

Rallycross – with extremely lightweight race-tuned saloons running on part-road/part-rough circuits essentially for the TV cameras, became a growing European sport as the 1970s progressed.

Autocross Drivers. These two forms of motor sport are effectively very short-distance racing; Rallycross operating on part-surfaced, part-unsurfaced circuits and Autocross taking place wholely 'on the rough'. These events are fun to watch and fun to participate in, and are largely the realm of an enthusiastic bunch of amateurs who produce some surprisingly sophisticated machinery to tackle their chosen sport.

5 Race Organisation

As race spectators flock to a circuit to see a major meeting, they may sit in traffic queues fuming while car parking snarls are put right. Paying at the circuit admission gates they take their tickets and programmes, make their way to their chosen vantage-point or grandstand seat, and settle down to witness a day's motor sport. Very few will arrive in time to see everything which happens in what is always a long hard day for those involved with the organisation of the meeting, and even fewer will ever think about what has gone on behind the scenes to make that day's sport happen. Race organisation is truly the unseen labour of any event.

Major meetings are slotted into the international calendar published some time before the start of each succeeding season by the international body, the FIA. Minor national and club meetings – and specialised events like American track races – do not concern this authority, and are handled purely by the national club, e.g. in Britain's case, the RAC whose race committee vets applications by would-be organising clubs, and shuffles their meetings into a carefully arranged calendar, allotting dates, times, perhaps Championship status in various classes, and the services of top officials, such as judges' stewards, scrutineers and timekeepers.

Pierre Aumonier, Competitions Secretary of the British Racing Drivers Club, explains some of the background to his organisation's International Trophy meeting of 1977 by going as far back as February 1976 when the BRDC applied to the RAC for a qualifying round in the European Formula 2 Championship. This application, together with other BRDC tenders for rounds in the World Championship of Makes and the European Touring Car and Formula 3 Championships was then forwarded by the RAC to the Parisian headquarters of the FIA, where applications from national bodies around the world were being collated into a draft International Sporting Calendar.

The various national interests often haggle over dates and Championship division before a final agreement is reached, after which the calendar is finalised, dates are awarded and detail organisation and planning may begin. Widely-travelled Championships, such as the Formula 2 and Touring Car competitions, have their own international committees who each meet twice a year to promote the uniform management of their Championship qualifying rounds in each individual country. It would be no good at all if BMW should receive preferential treatment in the German round, Jaguar or Triumph receive an advantage in Britain and the Autodelta team Alfa Romeo's have a two-lap start at Monza!

Once the form of the main event has been decided, fixing its allotted practice periods and race distance, the nature of the meeting's supporting events will be discussed. A balanced programme contrasting single-seater and enclosed-wheel racing is usually considered the optimum crowd-drawer, and once a complete programme has been finalised the supplementary regulations for the meeting are drafted and submitted to the national body – the RAC in this case – for their approval and the issue of a race permit.

Since international regulations for the Formula 2 Championship demanded that each round's regulations should be published three months before the event, entries opened for the 1977 International Trophy on 1st December 1976.

While Formula 2 teams ponder the regulations and place their entries in advance, the organising club has – as a matter of course – provided all its officials with an availability questionnaire. A list of available officials is then drawn up to check that an adequate number is available to guarantee that the meeting in question is properly manned. Simultaneously, the club's Chief Scrutineer and Chief Timekeeper arrange their teams for the coming season to match the type of meetings listed and the number of entries expected at each. For long-distance races such as the Silverstone

Six-hours endurance event, timekeepers have a massive task to keep track of the cars, and the scrutineers (whose main job is to ensure each car complies with the regulations) have to supervise all pit-stops and refuelling to ensure they are conducted as the regulations demand.

This section of the organiser's work is a matter of course, and his major meetings dovetail into the general work demanded by the whole season's calendar of meetings both large and small. Entries for the international event close one month prior to race day and a selection committee then picks those it will accept and those which will be offered a place merely as reserve entries should trouble strike those better established. In the case of a Championship-qualifying round, priority is given to points scorers in the competition and the remaining places are awarded to give a balanced entry, with as many different chassis, engines and nations represented as is possible. Qualifying heats and/or the provision of a main race split into two parts offers extra room for a massive entry to be accepted, but there are obvious practical limitations which mean some entrants may be disappointed.

Once the entry has been finalised its details, together with those of the meeting's events and its officials, are compiled into a programme and put out for printing. Advertising and pre-race publicity are arranged, and often there are meeting sponsors to be found to spread the organisers' financial burden. All professional teams contesting a recognised international championship are paid on an accepted scale.

Two weeks before the meeting, final instructions to competitors and officials are printed and despatched together with the appropriate passes to ensure easy entry to the circuit and to their appropriate places of work. Misfortune and misjudgement between the time that entries close and the day the meeting starts always create problems as some teams withdraw and reserve entries are then brought in to fill the gap. Every effort is made to fill vacant spaces to ensure a full entry for every race.

All this time, the promoter's publicity machine is churning out copy for the specialist magazines, national press and broadcasting media to keep the motor racing public informed. In the final reckoning it is the race spectator who makes motor racing possible at anything beyond the most modest club level, and spectators must be attracted at all costs.

In the case of the British 1977 International Trophy race, the BRDC as the organising club and Silverstone Circuit Ltd as the circuit company shared premises on the former airfield site, and while the club personnel organised the meeting itself, the circuit company prepared the course to receive spectators, provide their tickets, catering, grandstand or terrace accommodation, signposting, commentators, first aid, police assistance and emergency services. A million activities accompany every public event, and none happen by chance – each one has to be discussed, planned and arranged in advance.

When the morning of first practice dawns, the organising Secretary of the meeting hands over responsibility to the appointed Clerk of the Course who heads, in the case of this Silverstone international meeting, a staff of some 800 officials, in addition to the crowd facility team under the circuit company's direction.

The Clerk of the Course's executive party operates from the Race Control Office while the meeting is in progress, being linked by telephone to observers posted on every corner, to the paddock office where the race cars are undergoing final preparation, and to such officials as the Secretary of the Meeting, the Chief Scrutineer, Chief Paddock Marshal, Chief Pit Marshal, Chief Timekeeper, the Medical HQ and its staff of doctors, and to all emergency services.

Every major race circuit worth its salt has an internal roadway system which allows emergency services to concentrate on any part of the course very rapidly and without recourse to the track itself. Interestingly since passive safety measures have been widely adopted, such as mesh wire catch-fencings to trap cars which leave the road on corners, an extra problem has reared its head, for those torn-down fences must be replaced after an accident before the next event can be started. At Silverstone, a special repair team is in radio contact with the Clerk of the Course and is trained for rapid repair work immediately the practice session or race is ended. In this way delays to the scheduled programme can be minimised.

In the USA, where major-league racing is concentrated so much on the regularly-shaped oval tracks and speedways, and where even the largest Superspeedway measures no more than $2\frac{1}{2}$ miles round, emergency services may be even more efficiently organised. At Indianapolis and Ontario Motor Speedway, for example, it has been known for crane-equipped and fire-fighting trucks to meet a crashing car before the debris and wheels have stopped flying!

While in a trouble-free situation the Clerk of the Course and his Race Control staff will concentrate upon running their practice and race programme on time, the Secretary of the Meeting's Race Administration centre will be fully occupied producing information bulletins for use by the commentators, by the press and by

Clutches bite, wheels spin and another major race is under way. Here in 1965 Jackie Stewart, Richie Ginther, Graham Hill and Jimmy Clark charge away at Silverstone.

the competitors. These will list details of practice times, programme changes, and of course race progress and result information. This office also handles the innumerable queries which competitors, press and public alike will pose during the meeting. Information presented in the office's bulletins will be gathered from the Chief Timekeeper, from the Race Log maintained by telephone personnel in touch with observer posts out on the circuit who report incidents during practice or the race, and from the Chief Pit Marshal who logs all pit visits.

For major events attended by overseas newsmen, a hastily-scribbled interim bulletin is provided immediately the race finishes. This enables them to telephone or Telex immediate race stories to their publications or agencies, after which a full race bulletin will be produced and printed in numbers sufficient for all who require it. This is a function of the Secretary of the Meeting working jointly with his Press Officer, and its efficiency varies prodigiously from venue to venue, country to country, and sometimes from year to year. Few information services match those offered in the USA, however, where press offices gush out a mind-boggling profusion of information throughout the duration of a meeting, and often have full results available in bulk, timed to three decimal places, before the winning driver has drunk his champagne!

Another duty of the Secretary of the Meeting, which can often be an irritating one, is the signing-on and documentation of competitors. An experienced Secretary, like Aumonier at Silverstone, tells amazing stories of how so many competitors invest tens of thousands of pounds on cars, engines, transport, team personnel and travelling, and still arrive for an important race having forgotten their documentation. The arrival of a 'name' driver, upon whose presence the meeting's publicity has been founded, without his licence and medical certificate can leave the organisers in a ticklish situation . . .

Once the meeting has been completed, hopefully without undue disaster, the organising club pays out prize money as dictated by the Championship scale to the successful competitors. Where foreign teams are concerned this is done on race day immediately

The spectators' viewpoint, as at Brands Hatch during the wing era of 1968. Stand accommodation and the stadium-style view are similar today but the rickety pit row has long-since been demolished and replaced by a vast new complex in deference to constructors' pressure.

after the mandatory protest period – during which an aggrieved rival can place a fee to protest the race results. Other bills must be settled to close the accounts of the meeting, and its official results are then submitted to the national body – in this case the RAC, and the FIA makes note of the Championship points awarded to whichever competitors were successful.

Thereupon the race meeting passes into history and into the memories of those spectators, officials and competitors who were present. By this time the international and national calendars for the coming year are already being finalised, and the wheel is whirling round to bring along the next instalment in motor racing's never-ending serial.

6 Racing in Britain

Motor racing is at its most active and varied in Britain. Every summer weekend will see races of all kinds being held at circuits like Brands Hatch in Kent, Silverstone in Northamptonshire,

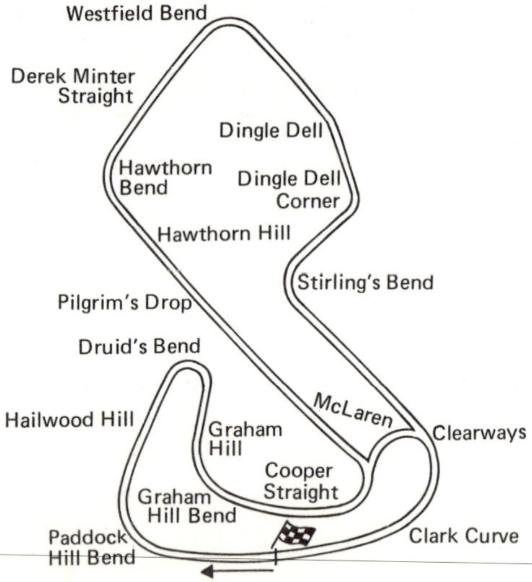

Brands Hatch, England.

Thruxton in Hampshire, Snetterton in Norfolk, Croft in Yorkshire and Mallory Park and Donington Park in Leicestershire.

The national governing body is the Royal Automobile Club's Motor Sports Division, based in London's Grosvenor Square, and this body sanctions various organising clubs to run meetings on these circuits; by arrangement with each individual circuit owner or promoter. One concern, Motor Circuit Developments Ltd, controls the Brands Hatch, Snetterton, Mallory Park and Oulton Park circuits. The RAC itself takes responsibility for the

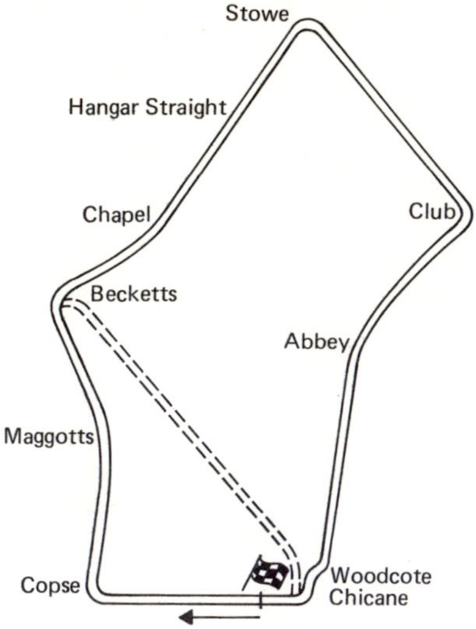

Silverstone, England.

annual World Championship qualifying British Grand Prix meeting, which in recent years has alternated between Brands Hatch and Silverstone, but in this case it draws heavily on experienced personnel from more active race-organising bodies to act as marshals, time-keepers, judges, observers, etc.

Prominent among Britain's race organising clubs are the British Racing & Sports Car Club, which grew out of the immediately postwar 500-cc racing movement, and which is based today at Brands Hatch. A slightly smaller organisation is the British Automobile Racing Club based at Thruxton, while the most select of them all is the British Racing Drivers' Club, which owns and operates the Silverstone circuit.

In recent years, the national governing body's race committee, which includes representatives from each of these clubs, has sanctioned a growing list of club racing Formulae in which competitors may chase a bewildering range of championships, some centred on one particular circuit and others organised into a series around the country's race venues.

Classes of Racing

Briefly, British club racing caters for the following classes, starting with the most prestigious:

Group 8 – Otherwise known as Formula 1, organised into a national Championship with some success in 1977 and catering for drivers in obsolete Grand Prix racing machinery using full 3-litre engines. Vehicles from the defunct 5-litre production-engined single-seater Formula 5000 class were also admitted, but they proved no match for the better-driven 3-litre racing-engined cars. Unfortunately, this proved to be more a class for drivers on their way down from Formula 1, than as the training ground it was intended to be for drivers on their way up.

Formula Atlantic – A national Formula also seen in slightly different form in North America – where it began – South Africa, Australasia and the Far East, demanding single-seater cars similar to those used in international Formula 2 but with production-based engines not exceeding 1,600-cc capacity. Supercharging and fuel-injection are banned, no more than five forward ratios may be used in the gearbox and minimum weight is just over 453 kg. In Britain, tyres are restricted to a specified type.

Formula Ford 2,000 – This big brother of the standard Formula Ford single-seater class admits 2-litre single overhead camshaft Ford engines, with certain modifications, not including the replacement of the standard inlet manifold and single carburettor. Potentially expensive monocoque chassis are banned, there is a maximum of four forward gears permitted and tyre choice is strictly defined. Minimum weight is 440 kg.

Formula Ford 1,600 – The now classical schoolroom single-seater class which began life in Britain in 1967 and has since spread throughout the racing world. Aerodynamic aids are banned, as are monocoque chassis, and the standard Ford 1,600-cc GT engine is demanded. Very limited and strictly observed modifications may be made to the engine, the idea being to keep the class economical. Restrictions help, limiting owners to no more than four forward gears and just one type of tyre. Minimum weight is 400 kg.

Formula Vee – This American-developed Formula uses the Volkswagen 1,300-cc (Type 1) engine and suspension within single-seat slipper-type bodies, and rapidly gained ground in Europe during the 1960s when imported by US servicemen. Aerodynamic aids are banned and with a minimum weight of 375 kg the Formula is a European equivalent of Formula Ford 1,600, but has produced fewer graduates to Formula 1.

Formula Super Vee – An international Formula contested on club level in the UK using Volkswagen engines not exceeding 1,600 cc. Modifications are permitted, chassis construction is unrestricted and aerodynamic aids of limited size are legal. There is a maximum allowance of four forward speeds within a Volkswagen transmission case. Minimum weight is 400 kg.

Formula 4 – Yet another single-seater class on true enthusiast level with a small, and relatively impecunious following, catering for racing single-seaters using Ford, British Leyland or Chrysler engines up to 1,000 cc or Ford pushrod overhead valve engines up to 1,300 cc. Fuel injection is banned but there are no chassis restrictions and aerodynamic aids are permitted.

Monoposto Formula – The foot of the ladder in 'poor man's' single-seater club racing, open to either production racing chassis built prior to 30th September 1970, or to home-built chassis of any age. Maximum engine capacity is 1,600 cc but only pushrod overhead valve units are permitted since overhead camshaft engines and/or superchargers are banned on grounds of cost. Aerodynamic aids are permitted.

Group 1 Touring Cars – This is really an FIA international class catering for four-seat (or more) production saloon cars of which at least 5,000 identical units per year are produced. Very limited modifications are permitted, mostly on the grounds of safety, so that virtually all standard original equipment has to be retained. In Britain, the RAC's liberalised version of Group 1 varies from the international Formula in allowing more freedom in the choice of 'optional extras', the use of racing in place of road tyres, the provision of limited-slip differentials even where they are not offered by the original vehicle manufacturer, and choice of springs and dampers is free. Safety equipment regulations are more stringent than those applied by the FIA. This class contests the annual British Touring Car Championship in four sub-divisions, decided on engine capacity: up to 1,300 cc; 1,301–1,600 cc; 1,601–2,500 cc; and 2,501–3,000 cc. Engine displacements of above 3,000 cc are not permitted, since American large-capacity V8-engined cars once dominated British saloon car racing.

Group 2 Touring Cars – This is one step further up the FIA's international production saloon car racing ladder, catering for more select vehicles of which only 1,000 per year may have been produced. Extensive modifications, far in excess of Group 1's, are permitted to improve the vehicles' competition capabilities. Engine components may be extensively balanced and machined, cockpits may be gutted for light weight and extensive suspension and transmission modifications may be made providing the vehicle retains its standard basic components and its external shape remains unaltered above hub height. Wide wheels up to 16 inches are permitted, and this potent division is that adopted by the FIA European Touring Car Championship, in which BMW and Ford Cologne competed notably in recent years.

Special Saloons – This is the Group 8 of the closed-car world in which much-modified racing cars carry bodyshells of vaguely familiar shape to road car buffs. This is a national British category which permits huge scope for modification so long as the general shape of the chosen production car remains unchanged, the driver is seated on the same side as the original and the engine, clutch and gearbox remain in the *same end* of the car as designed by its manufacturer! The type of final drive and its position is free and aerodynamic aids like air dams and spoilers are permitted. The class is subdivided to cater for engines of up to 850 cc; 851–1,000 cc; 1,001–1,300 cc; 1,301–2,500 cc; and over 2,500 cc. Supercharged and turbocharged engines have their capacity judged at 1·4 times its nominal displacement. Hybrid saloons abound, using Formula 1 Cosworth V8 engines in something looking like a Volkswagen, or Chevrolet V8 engines in 'Ford Capris'.

Production Saloons – Yet another saloon car class but this time with no optional extras permitted, running on road tyres though with freedom for the replacement of standard dampers and exhaust systems, improvement to engine lubrication arrangements and reduction of both vehicle weight and ground clearance. A national class which sees Fords, BMWs, Opels, even Moskvitches racing while looking 'just like you can buy' without the expensive restriction-dodging found in 'Group 1½' and the British Saloon Car Championship.

One Make Formulae – Various championships are organised every year for Ford Escort Sports or Renault 5TSs, in which races are run purely for cars of this type. Others include the Mini 850, 1,000 and 1,275 GT – all good fun at club level with the accent on driver ability.

Sports 2000 – A relatively new national Formula introduced in 1977, and catering for open two-seat sports-racing cars using the Ford 2-litre overhead camshaft engine as employed in Formula Ford 2,000. Chassis design and construction is virtually free but aerodynamic aids are restricted, the bodyshell must cover all mechanical components in plan form and tyres are limited to a specified type.

Modified Sports – The famous and popular 'ModSports' class caters for production-based sports and GT cars subdivided into – 1 up to 1,150 cc; 1,151–1,500 cc; 1,501–2,000 cc and over 2,000 cc. Each season's RAC 'Blue Book' of regulations specifies the models of car to be recognised. Modifications are restricted although aerodynamic aids are allowed if the original shape of the car is retained, manifolds and carburettors are free, the engine's cubic capacity may be increased to its class limit and they may also be supercharged or turbocharged, although they then carry a 40 per cent capacity loading, so moving the vehicle up a class.

Clubmans Sports – A national and supremely well-supported and potent division, whose performance belies the rather quaint appearance of the cars with their cycle mudguards and offset driving positions. The regulations demand open two-seat front-engined sports chassis with cycle-type wings, arranged in two classes; up to 1,600 cc fully-modified, or Formula Ford 1,600-limited power units. The free-modification engines must be of overhead valve pushrod-operated type made by British Leyland, Ford of Dagenham, Chrysler UK or General Motors UK. Wheels and tyres are free and aerodynamic aids are permitted.

Production Sports – Known inevitably as 'ProdSports' this class demands production sports and GT cars divided into three sections defined by an RAC list of eligible models. This list of recognised models is revised each year, keeping in step with current production cars which must be raced in un-modified form excluding options offered to improve their handling, performance and weight. Permitted modifications are as for Production Saloons.

Formula 1,300 – More 'poor man's motor racing' which can prove remarkably rapid. A national Formula for two-seat sports-racing cars using either the Ford pushrod overhead valve 1,200-cc engine in up to 1,222-cc form, or the standard Ford 1,300-cc engine. Only chassis restriction is one demanding that no production rear-engined model built later than January 1971 may be used.

Formula 750 – 'Poor man's motor racing' at its original shoestring level evolved immediately after World War II with 750 Motor Club members building sports cars around Austin 7 chassis and their side-valve four-cylinder engines. Colin Chapman's first Lotus and Eric Broadley's forerunner of the Lola line were both 750 Formula cars but today the class caters for two-seaters fitted with either the Reliant overhead-valve 748-cc engine or the Reliant 747-cc side-valve and Austin side-valve units, which may be either front or rear mounted in their chassis. Regulations are carefully framed to minimise costs, and still 750 MC members prove remarkably inventive, and their cars remarkably rapid.

The Historic Classes – Naturally nostalgia-minded Britons love to race their historic and vintage cars and in recent years an economy level of even this type of competition has developed. While the Vintage Sports Car Club is extremely active in organising race meetings for its Edwardian (pre-1914), Vintage (1919–30) and Post-Vintage (1930–39) car owners, it also caters for true racing cars of all ages up to 1960 (and the demise of the front-engined layout). Regular races are also held by a variety of organisations catering for postwar Historic Sports Cars, Classic Sports and GT cars such as Ford GT40s and Lola T70GTs, Thoroughbred Sports Cars of the 1950s, Classic Saloons like 3·8 Jaguars, Ford Zephyrs and Austin A35s of the 1950s, and even for Formula 3 500-cc cars and Formula Junior single-seaters. Basically no racing car today is valueless, for around the corner there is always the possibility of a new class opening up to revive it!

7 Racing in the USA

American motor racing lives half a world away from its predominantly European-based road racing counterpart. Circuit racing is quite well-established in the USA, but still it plays second fiddle to track racing, from the most minor indoor midget-car venue to the gigantic Indianapolis Motor Speedway in Indiana and the stock car racing 'Super Speedways' of the Deep South.

American motor racing has its own history and has developed independently of what we may call mainstream road racing. It was track-race orientated from an early time, and when Brooklands Motor Course opened in Britain in 1907, a group of Indianapolis businessmen were attracted to the idea of a big, permanent speedway. At that time small dirt-tracks were proliferating around their nation, and most fairgrounds staged auto races as a titillating, death-defying and carefully staged side-show.

Carl G. Fisher was prime mover behind the Indianapolis Motor Speedway project and he launched the construction of the rectangular 2½-mile course in 1908. The first races were run there, controversially, in 1909 when the original surface material broke up, and the Speedway was subsequently brick-paved to earn its nickname, 'The Brickyard'. In 1911, the first 500-Miles Sweepstake race was run, starting a series which has continued (broken only by the war years of 1917–18 and 1942–5) to the present day.

The race was promoted with a first prize (and later a prize fund) huge by European standards and rapidly established itself as the world's richest motor race. Typically American in its hard-sell promotion, the Indy '500' is the shining example of what could be done with such a permanent facility, and such an individual annual motor race.

On a subsidiary level to this great speedway classic, racing was progressing along other lines in the USA. William K. Vanderbilt promoted his Vanderbilt Cup road race – Grand Prix-style – on Long Island from 1904, while on 18th June that year Packard designer/driver Charles Schmidt attempted to run 1,000 miles without switching off his engine on the dirt track at Grosse Pointe. He crashed after 228 miles. Later that year, with two relief drivers, Schmidt ran 820 miles in 24 hours and passed the 1,000-mile mark almost six hours later. In May 1905 the rival Peerless concern bettered Packard's figures when Charles Wridgeway ran 923 miles in one day, and then Guy Vaughan put these performances in perspective with a 1902 Decauville 40 racer in which he put 1,015 miles into 24 hours. In November 1905, 'Jap' Clemens and a young Charlie Merz drove their National over 1,094 miles in 24 hours to set the seal on this brief period of record breaking.

USA Grand Prize racing represented the height of American road race endeavour before the First World War. Here at Savannah in 1911 is Ralph de Palma in E. H. Schroeder's Mercedes 'Grey Ghost'.

The Columbus Auto Club of Ohio had meanwhile been prompted by these attempts to run a 'motor marathon' for stripped stock (production) cars. The Soules brothers won in a Pope-Toledo, covering 828·5 miles in the 24 hours allocated. In May 1907 the age of the 24-hour 'grinds' as they were known began at Point Breeze horse track, Pennsylvania and with the showman management of Bill Pickens these awe-inspiring dices with death provided great entertainment (for the period) and good business. Other 'grinds' were organised in succeeding seasons, at Detroit, Chicago, Saint Paul, Brighton Beach and Morris Park in New York, Birmingham, Seattle, Milwaukee and Los Angeles. The last 24-hour grind of this remarkable series was held on the Brighton Beach dirt track in August 1910, when a small crowd saw Al Poole and Cyrus Patschke setting a record 1,253-mile distance in Jack Rutherford's Stearns.

Meanwhile European-style road racing embraced the American Grand Prize inaugurated at Savannah, Georgia, in 1908 and run again in 1910–11, then at various other circuits such as Milwaukee, Santa Monica and San Francisco into 1916. Road races were also organised at Briarcliff, New York, Lowell, Massachusetts, and Fairmount Park, Philadelphia, and at Portland, Crown Point, Denver, Oakland, Cincinatti, Bakersfield, Tacoma, San Diego and Corona among other venues. In many of these events imported European cars did well against the home product, but slowly the emphasis grew upon enclosed short-lap oval tracks. As early as 1908, Asa Chandler and Ed Durant had built a gravel-surfaced two-mile oval track at Atlanta and simultaneously, over on the West Coast, a businessman named Fred Moscovics was having his own ideas on speedway design. He had been educated for a time in Zürich, Switzerland, and cycle racing on wooden *vélodromes* had fascinated him. He came to know many of the top racing cyclists, including the British-born World Champion, Jack Prince. When Prince retired from competition he emigrated to the States and established a business designing and building one-eighth and quarter-mile board tracks for cycle racing. As motor-cycles gained popularity, Prince accommodated them on half-mile board tracks and – when Moscovics went into partnership with a retired racing driver named Fred Gurbut to build an Indy-style oval in California – they chose a monster version of Prince's wooden Velodrome.

This timber speedway was relatively cheap and quick to build and on 8th April 1910, the world's first one-mile board speedway was opened just outside Los Angeles at Playa del Rey. It was perfectly circular, 45 ft wide and banked 15 ft high around the outer rim. Gurbut put steel crash rails around the lip and 'The Great Wooden Wonder of Playa del Rey' cost its promoters $85,000 to construct, including floodlighting to stage the sensational spectacle of night racing.

This Los Angeles Motordrome drew 15,000 spectators a day, proved very fast and was as safe as one could possibly expect with the cars and hard-nosed drivers of the time. Disaster came in 1913, when the Wooden Wonder burned to the ground, but promoters across the nation had got the message and other board speedways sprang up near any likely centre of population. Some were enormous structures – like the two-mile ovals at Sheepshead Bay in Brooklyn, and the Chicago and Tacoma tracks. They were ovals with parallel straights joined by 180-degree banked turns super-elevated as much as 45 degrees.

The gravel track at Atlanta had flopped while the board speedways went from strength to strength. A total of twenty-four board tracks were built in America from 1910 and they survived in ever more fragile condition until 1931. They decided the definitive form of the American racing car. Here there was no demand for braking, cornering and handling in the sophisticated road racing sense. Here speed was the aim, pure and simple, and engine development and minimal aerodynamic frontal area were all important. Highly supercharged engines were developed by Miller and others which ran reliably for anything up to 500 miles absolutely flat-out – mounted in slender chassis frames carrying slim, classically simple single-seater central-seat bodyshells when the regulations allowed.

Many of the successful speedway cars owed the initiation of their development to the European racing practise of 1914, shipped to America when World War I broke out, in the form of the Peugeots in which English-Italian Dario Resta dominated the 1915 American road and track racing season. The duels of 1916 were notable for Resta's Peugeot battle with Ralph de Palma's Grand Prix Mercedes, while Johnny Aitken was another to shine in a French-built Peugeot.

The lessons of this four-valve per cylinder, twin overhead camshaft design and of the similar Ballot which followed postwar were quickly learned. By 1917 Stutz, Frontenac, Peerless and Miller were winning races regularly and in 1919 Tommy Milton began winning for Duesenberg – who two years later took home the *GP de l'ACF* trophy from Le Mans.

Through the 1920s and early 1930s if a driver had one of Harry Miller's cars in speedway racing he was in good shape. American track racing had grown a world away from European-style road racing, and in many respects was far in advance of European technical developments.

Track racing became 'The Thing' in America between the Wars as here in the early 1920s with the beautifully prepared Stutz team up front flanked by Ballot.

1 Classic cars, classic circuit: five great racing cars at Britain's Donington Park racing circuit on its reopening in 1977. They are 1939 Multi-Union (driven by Hermann Lang), 1934 Maserati 8CM, 1955 Mercedes-Benz, 1934 Alfa Romeo and 1914 French GP-winning Mercedes.

2 Shape of the 1920s as America's 1961 World Champion driver Phil Hill puts a 1921 3-litre GP Sunbeam through its paces at Donington Park, 1977.

3 The immortal Alfa Romeo Tipo B *Monoposto* of the early 1930s was the first successful Grand Prix single-seater to place its driver on the centre-line.

4 German state assistance brought Daimler-Benz and Auto Union to pre-eminence in the late 1930s with cars like this 1937 Mercedes-Benz W125 whose 5.66-litre supercharged 8-cylinder engine – at 600-horsepower or more – was the most powerful in Grand Prix history.

5 Assistance from industry produced the centrifugally-supercharged $1\frac{1}{2}$-litre V1 6 cylinder BRM of the early 1950s which promised much but delivered little until the Formula to which it was built had died. Still its specific output of 500bhp-plus from only 1500cc has not been surpassed.

6 Juan Fangio, World Champion for Alfa Romeo in 1951 demonstrates one of the glorious *Alfettas* at Monaco during the 1960s. Behind him in a later car is Giuseppe Farina, first ever World Champion in 1950.

7 The car which toppled the supercharged 1½-litre *Alfetta* from its throne in 1951 was the 4½-litre unsupercharged V12-cylinder Ferrari 375. Here an Indianapolis version of this car is demonstrated at Long Beach, 1976.

8 Italian red once more, on the works Maserati 250F driven by Sergio Mantovani in the 1954 Spanish GP at Barcelona's public road Pedralbes circuit. Maseratis helped Fangio to two of his record five World Championships, in 1954 and 1957.

9 and 10 German silver as shown on the 1954 streamlined version of the Mercedes-Benz W196 *(above)* and on the later slipper-bodied variant which raced on into 1955 *(below)*, carrying Juan Fangio to World titles both seasons. Pre-war Champion Hermann Lang drives at Dijon 1975 while Fangio tries his hand at Long Beach 1976.

11 Mercedes-Benz also dominated sports car racing in 1955 with Stirling Moss and writer Denis Jenkinson scoring their most noble triumph in the incredible round-Italy Mille Miglia. Here Moss demonstrates one of the team's 300SLR sports models on the public road.

12 Deadly rival of Mercedes-Benz – particularly at Le Mans – was the classic D-Type Jaguar which won the 24-Hour race in 1955, 1956 and 1957, its 3.4-litre 6-cylinder engine punching the car up to 180–190mph on the long Mulsanne Straight.

13 Rare shot of a rare car: Cooper popularised mid-mounted engines in Grand Prix cars. Here Englishman Bob Gerard demonstrates the style in his 6-cylinder Bristol-powered device, 1956.

14 How it was, 1957: the full might of Scuderia Ferrari's V8-cylinder team lined up before the Aintree pits during British GP practice, with Maserati beyond. This race was the writing on the wall for Italian domination, as Stirling Moss and Tony Brooks shared the winning Vanwall for Britain.

15 Teardrop: the British-built Vanwall which began winning GP races In 1957 and stole the World Formula 1 Manufacturers' Championship in 1958. Stuart Lewis-Evans driving here was tragically killed in one of the cars in the deciding race of the 1958 season.

16 Britain's BRM team tackled $2\frac{1}{2}$-litre racing from 1955 to 1959 with front-engined 4-cylinder cars like this replica P25, seen here with Historic Car Champion Nell Corner driving at Donington Park, 1974.

17 Blacksmith's job: the mid-engined Cooper-Climax cars were crude specials in comparison to the front-engined craftsmanship found in Vanwall and BRM, but they out-performed them all. Here Jack Brabham wins the French GP at Reims, 1960.

18 Not all Ferraris have been red. In the 1961 Belgian GP at Spa, national Champion Olivier Gendebien drove this works Tipo 156 in his country's yellow racing colours, and completed a team 1-2-3-4 finish.

19 Even in 1962 with the $1\frac{1}{2}$-litre 'kiddy car' Formula you could see the drivers at work. Here Lorenzo Bandini concentrates hard in his Ferrari, leaving the Station Hairpin, Monaco.

20 Le Mans has always been important. Here Ferrari's armada prepares in a local garage prior to the 1963 24-Hour classic.

21 Jim Clark supreme: here the double-World Champion's Lotus-Climax leads Bandini, Stewart, Gurney, Surtees, Ginther and Amon into the first turn at the Charade circuit, Clermont-Ferrand in the 1965 French GP. He won – of course.

22 Story of the $1\frac{1}{2}$-litre years, Graham Hill (BRM) versus Jim Clark (Lotus-Climax) – the scene at Monaco, 1965 when Hill notched his hat-trick of victories and Clark failed to finish.

RODO
4
21

23 Aviator: Clark again, this time in the first Cosworth-Ford DFV-powered 3-litre Lotus 49 with all wheels off the track at the German GP, Nurburgring, 1967.

24 Victory for the USA, the first since Jimmy Murphy's Duesenberg won the French GP in 1921, came at Spa-Francorchamps in 1967 when Dan Gurney's V12 All-American Eagle won the Belgian GP.

25 American success story of another sort: Jim Hall's winged Chaparral 2F long-distance car revolutionised motor racing aerodynamics. But here at Sicily's Targa Florio, 1967, with Hap Sharp driving, it was out of its element.

26 Jackie Stewart, driving the Tyrrell Matra-Ford, British GP 1968, finished an exhausted sixth with a broken wrist in plaster. In 1969, in a developed car, he would win his first World Championship.

27 Tragic Champion: Jochen Rindt in the trend-setting Lotus 72 at Jarama, Spain in 1970. He crashed fatally at Monza later that year, but nobody could better his points total.

28 Pastoral scene of racing as it has been in recent history, with Jacky Ickx's 1970 Ferrari on the public-road Spa-Francorchamps circuit for the Belgian GP.

29 Monsters at Le Mans: two of Porsche's hyper-streamlined 5-litre flat-12 917Ls slam past a 180mph Ferrari Daytona on their way towards 235mph at the Sarthe, another public road circuit, in 1971.

30 The youngest World Champion: Brazilian Emerson Fittipaldi took the 1972 title at the age of 25 in this John Player Special Lotus 72. Here at Monza in 1973 he dives beneath the camera to enter the Curva Parabolica.

31 Record-breaker: Jackie Stewart in his Tyrrell 006/2 wins the Dutch GP at Zandvoort, 1973, and sets an all-time record of 27 Championship Grand Prix victories . . . and is set for his third World title.

32 Classic start: the French GP grid at Ricard-Castellet, 1971. Ready to go are Jackie Stewart's Tyrrell, the Ferraris of Clay Regazzoni and Jacky Ickx, and behind them Graham Hill's Brabham and Pedro Rodriguez's BRM.

33 Getaway: the 1978 Brazilian GP gets under way at the new Rio de Janeiro circuit with James Hunt's McLaren leading Ronnie Peterson's Lotus 78, Mario Andretti's 78 and Carlos Reutemann's winning Ferrari.

34 First corners can be all important. Here, at Long Beach in 1976, this initial ess-bend proved tricky in the extreme, but the TV viewers had a good view (see camera on left).

35 Sometimes even the aces get it wrong. Here, in the 1977 Belgian GP at Zolder, Mario Andretti punted John Watson's Brabham-Alfa up the tail on the opening lap and put both cars out of the race.

36 Racing 'line' clearly demonstrated here at Monte Carlo 1976 as cars stream away from Mirabeau Inferieur into the Portier.

37 The glamour of Grand Prix racing pictured at Monaco's Old Station Hairpin, 1977. Jody Scheckter's winning Wolf leads from Watson's Brabham-Alfa, Reutemann's Ferrari, Stuck's Brabham-Alfa, Peterson's Tyrrell, Lauda's Ferrari and Hunt's McLaren, and there is nowhere to overtake. . .

GITANES
TEXACO
Marlboro
MARTINI
TEXACO
GITANES
Marlboro
Bendix
ZIEBART

38 and 39 Ess-bends demand perfect line as seen here at Watkins Glen *(above)* in the 1974 United States GP and at Sao Paulo's Interlagos circuit *(below)* in the 1977 Brazilian GP. Very different circuits, but the demands are similar.

40 and 41 'Progress' in Germany where the nation's Grand Prix was traditionally held at the Nurburgring *(above)* until 1976, after which it moved for safety reasons to Hockenheim *(below)* where it had been run once-off in 1970.

42 and 43 Incidents: the late Mark Donohue ends a minor Monaco incident against the outside barrier at Ste Devote (*above*) in 1975, while (*below*) Arturo Merzario and all those photographers escaped unharmed when the Williams vaulted Jarama's safety barrier the previous year. The dangling front wing caused this accident by lifting the car's nose!

44 Eastern promise: the mighty cone of Mount Fuji towers above Jacques Laffite's French Ligier-Matra and the twin Tyrrells of Patrick Depailler and Ronnie Peterson during the Japanese GP, 1977.

45 Grand Prix racing in the southern hemisphere: with Jean-Pierre Jarier's ATS leading Rupert Keegan's Surtees and Emerson Fittipaldi's Brazilian Copersucar during the 1978 Argentine GP in the Park at Buenos Aires.

46 Racing in the rain: Hans-Joachim Stuck's Brabham-Alfa Romeo streams past the Zolder pits during the Belgian GP 1977, its grooved wet-weather tyres furlously draining water.

47 South of the Equator: the South African GP field streams into Crowthorne Corner at Kyalami, 1977.

48 Grand Prix shapes, one: Jacques Laffite's French Ligier is powered by the Matra-Simca 3-litre V12 engine which once dominated Le Mans.

49 Grand Prix shapes, two: a British sponsorship special In the form of Rupert Keegan's Hesketh-Ford V8.

50 Grand Prix shapes, three: Patrick Depailler's sensational six-wheeled Tyrrell-Ford V8s ran with variable success in 1976-1977.

51 Grand Prix shapes, four: Mario Andretti's Lotus 78 'wing car' was the sensation of 1977 and was robbed of Championship honours by mid-season engine failures.

52 Renault won the very first Grand Prix in 1906 and returned to the fray in 1977 with the first 1½-litre turbocharged car to tackle 3-litre Formula 1. Here, at Silverstone, in its debut, driver Jean-Pierre Jabouille tried hard.

elf
FACOM
MICHELIN
RoT
FACOM

53 Leading driver of the late 1970s, Niki Lauda, in the Ferrari at Nurburgring for the 1976 German GP. Here in the Karussel turn, he later escaped death narrowly when the car crashed and burned.

54 Stolen crown: James Hunt pipped Lauda to the World Championship after the 1976 Nurburgring fire, but the Austrian came back to win again in 1977. Here in the 1977 British GP, Hunt won for McLaren.

55 and 56 The bustle and atmosphere of the Le Mans 24-Hour race in 1967 (*above*) and 1966 (*below*) as the cars assemble before the pits, then form up for the run and jump-style 'Le Mans start', now outlawed.

57 Pit work is an integral part of the fun in long-distance racing. Here Ferrari go to work at Le Mans in 1973, the flexible hose supplying compressed air to power a wheel-nut wrench.

58 Problem at Le Mans as one of the extremely fast Matra-Simcas which won the classic race in 1972, 1973 and 1974 closes up rapidly on far slower GT Porsches.

59 *Legion d'Honneur* holder Henri Pescarolo, three-times Le Mans winner for the French Matra-Simca team, at the Sarthe in 1974.

60 Spirit of long-distance racing as dusk settles on the Sarthe, the Goodyear blimp flies overhead, and sports-racing cars scream away from Mulsanne Corner into the night.

61 Spirit of the Targa Florio, where local villagers high in the Madonie Mountains of Sicily watch an Italian-red Alfa Romeo charge by on another 45-mile lap.

KONI

62 Spirit of NASCAR racing in America's deep south, as big-engined stock cars slipstream one another on a thunderous lap of the Daytona SuperSpeedway, Florida.

63 American in Formula 1: Mario Andretti in the unfortunate Vel's Parnelli Jones VPJ-Ford which he drove in Grand Prix racing in 1974-76. Ex-Lotus designer Maurice Phillippe is standing on the right.

64, 65 and 66 Spirit of Indianapolis with the famed portals of Gasoline Alley *(above left)*, massive crowds watching the tense build-up to the 500-Miles start *(above right)* and cars in their 220mph straightaway charge into the gently-banked turns *(below)*.

67 Texan A.J. Foyt's Coyote-Foyt/Ford V8 roars towards second place in the 1976 Indy '500' which was shortened due to rain, leaving Johnny Rutherford's McLaren to win. Foyt won in 1977 to take an unprecedented fourth '500' in 20 annual attempts.

68 Champion to Champion: Jackie Stewart, retired from Formula 1 racing, interviews USAC ace Bobby Unser for ABC TV's *Wide World of Sport* programme.

69 Another type of racing: BMWs like this one have dominated European Touring Car Championship racing on circuits such as the Nurburgring seen here.

70 Another type of racing: British club special saloons look like VWs and Ford Capris, but often pack Formula 1 V8 power units beneath the skin! Here they negotiate Red Gate Corner at Donington Park.

71 Another type of racing: Formula 3 single-seaters battle it out around the Old Station Hairpin at Monte Carlo in the most prestigious race of their year.

72 Yet another type of racing: historic Lotus cars leave the start-line in another British club event.

73 For something completely different, how about running a vintage Bentley in the trans-Continental World Cup Rally?

74 Serious rallying, with the purpose-built Lancia Stratos cornering hard on an unsurfaced forest track.

75, 76, 77 and 78 Grand Prix power plants ranging from the still-born 1½-litre flat-16-cylinder Coventry Climax unit of 1965 on test (*top left*), through the unsuccessful H16-cylinder BRM of 1966-67 (*centre*) and the gas-turbine powered Lotus 56B of 1971 (*bottom*) to the epoch-making 3-litre Cosworth-Ford DFV V8 of 1967-1978 (*top right*) (Plate 78). The V8 won seven consecutive World Championships from 1968-1974, lost the title to Ferrari in 1975.

79 Pre-First World War trend-setter: the 4-valve per cylinder twin overhead camshaft Peugeots set a race-winning fashion, still racing in 1978. This is Briggs Cunningham's car in California.

80 'Tween wars sophistication: the incredible 1½-litre 8-cylinder twin-camshaft Delage of 1926-27 won again in Dick Seaman's hands in 1936.

81 Sophistication in the 1970s: Ferrari's Championship-winning 3-litre flat-12 Tipo 312 engine gives 500 HP, yet is only knee-high.

82 The French Regle Renault broke new ground with this Francois Castaing-designed $1\frac{1}{2}$-litre turbocharged V6 F1 engine in 1977-78.

83, 84 and 85 Great drivers, different eras: wind-cheating jacket, flimsy crash helmet and plastic visor days as Juan Manuel Fangio *(above)* takes his Maserati out of the Aintree pits in 1957. Below *(left)* is the great Scot, Jimmy Clark, in a Formula 2 Lotus in 1965, with *(right)* his compatriot Jackie Stewart.

86, 87 and 88 Great drivers of the 1970s: (*above*) the Italian-born American Mario Andretti, with Colin Chapman of Lotus, is the greatest all-rounder the modern sport has ever known. Below *(right)* is Brazil's Emerson Fittipaldi, with *(left)* Sweden's uncrowned Champion, Ronnie Peterson.

89 and 90 The sensational season of 1976 will always be remembered for the duel between Niki Lauda of Austria *(left)* and James Hunt of Britain *(right)*.

91 and 92 The Belgian ace Jacky Ickx came closest to the World Championship in 1970, driving for Enzo Ferrari *(right)*, prominent in international racing since the 1920s.

93 Flashback to an era of strutted aerofoil aids and treaded dry-weather tyres at Rouen in 1968, where Graham Hill ponders his Lotus chances.

94 Strip-down before Le Mans with Cosworth-Ford V8-engined Gulf Mirage cars being meticulously prepared.

95 The hard graft behind the glamour in the pits at Silverstone 1977 as a Goodyear tyre technician checks temperatures on the six-wheeled Tyrrell's troublesome left-front – the tyre which conventional cars always lean on round clockwise race circuits.

96 and 97 Behind every ace driver there is a hard-worked team of mechanics and engineers providing his (or her) machinery. Here *(above)* we see a Ferrari monocoque chassis without its engine *(below)* which is about to be re-mounted.

98 Practice period, with discussions and adjustments going on around Clay Regazzoni's Ferrari and Vittorio Brambilla's March in 1974.

99 and 100 Startling comparison between the racing cockpit of a pre-World War One racer *(above)* and that of a modern McLaren Formula 1 car *(below)*. While there was space for a riding mechanic to travel with the driver in the TT Sunbeam, the McLaren pilot doesn't even have space for a 'proper' sized steering wheel. On the cockpit floor is the extinguisher bottle.

101 Safety equipment for the driver: James Hunt wears a typical flame-proofed balaclava beneath his visored crash helmet, with breathable air piped directly into it in the event of fire. A head restraint behind his helmet is a thoughtful feature of his car.

102 Preparing to do combat: the 1978 Parmalat Brabham-Alfa Romeos line-up prior to Argentine GP practice at Buenos Aires; John Watson on the right, Niki Lauda (fresh from Ferrari) on the left.

103 Strapped firmly into the cockpit of his 1972 World Championship-holding Lotus 72 is Emerson Fittipaldi, showing flameproofed overalls, gloves and face-mask.

104 Another World of racing: sprint cars on the dirt-oval at Tampa, Florida where close-quarter sideways racing is the order of the day.

105 Typical US sprint car is colourful, and to European eyes incredibly antiquated. The drivers are a tough breed and Mario Andretti – who should know – describes US sprint and midget racing as "the most educational I've ever done...'

106 Masked against flying gravel and sand, protected from roll-over injury by his seat belts and massive roll-cage, with nudge bars to prevent his rear wheels tangling with those on other cars, a sprinter prepares for war.

107 International flag signals: 1 National flag to start the race; 2 Car must stop at pits next time round; this flag is shown by race control (not the team), together with the car number; this is the U.S.A. version, known as the 'Meatball'; 3 British and European version of the same flag; 4 All cars must stop immediately, cease racing; 5 Hazard now removed, all clear; 6 Services vehicle or ambulance on track; 7 Held steady, caution; when waved, 'extreme caution, there has been an incident'; 8 Oil on track; 9 When held steady, 'another car is following you closely'; when waved, 'another car is trying to overtake you'; 10 Finish of race or practice session.

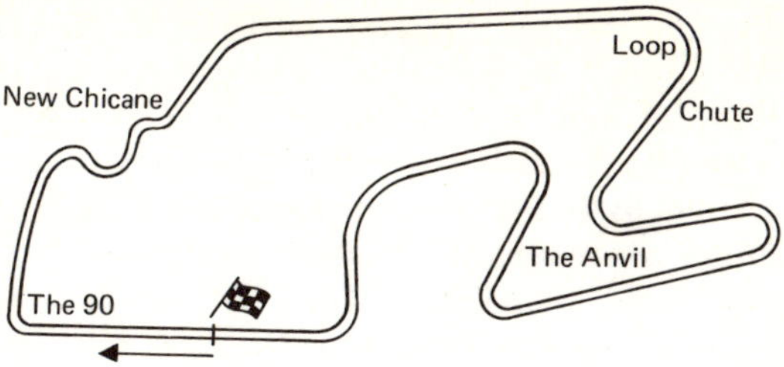

Watkins Glen, USA.

During the years of their decline the board speedway races were run in a continuous hail of splinters, and when larger holes appeared in the bankings carpenters would be working away repairing them while cars raced overhead! Dirt track and paved-oval racing took the board tracks' place in the 1930s, having played second fiddle in earlier years. A handful of hill-climb courses such as Pike's Peak, and the Climb to the Clouds at Mt Washington reminded some competition drivers how to turn right as well as left, and in the early 1930s a feeble road racing flame flared as the Elgin circuit was revived in Illinois and some events were run around Mines Field, the Los Angeles Municipal Airport. In 1936–7, a group of New York promoters staged two Vanderbilt Cup races on a specially-built Long Island circuit, and attracted entries from Alfa Romeo, Mercedes-Benz and Auto Union. Nuvolari won the first race in a Ferrari team Alfa, and the second running fell to Bernd Rosemeyer's V16-cylinder Auto Union. An amateur group of well-heeled enthusiasts formed the Automobile Racing Club of America (ARCA) which ran road-circuit races along very genteel lines, apparently as they fondly imagined Brooklands to be run in Britain. Some quite potent European road racing machinery was imported and raced on circuits like Alexandria Bay, Montauk Point and through the grounds of the 1940 New York World's Fair.

After the war road racing grew around a hard-core of surviving

ARCA members, and the Sports Car Club of America gained strength – very much on an amateur basis, in vivid contrast to those rough professional people on the oval tracks. An enthusiast named Cameron R. Argetsinger initiated racing around the streets of Watkins Glen in upper New York state in 1948. From this small beginning grew an out-of-town road course in the mid-1950s and eventually the artificial road course which first hosted the United States Grand Prix World Championship round in 1961, and which still accommodates the US Grand Prix (East) today.

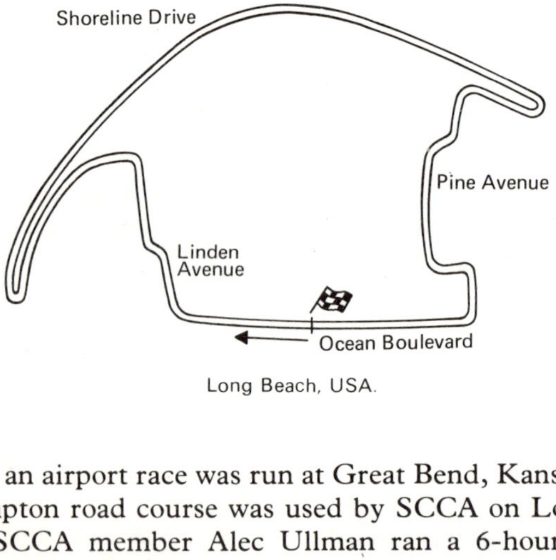

Long Beach, USA.

In 1949, an airport race was run at Great Bend, Kansas, and the Bridgehampton road course was used by SCCA on Long Island. In 1950, SCCA member Alec Ullman ran a 6-hour inaugural sports car race around Hendrick Air Base, Sebring, Florida and in 1952 this event was established as a 12-Hour endurance event. A year later it saw the opening round of the first World Sports Car Championship. Other road circuits followed, like Road America at Elkhart Lake, Wisconsin, Floyd Bennett airfield, Brooklyn, and many more air bases. By 1956 the short-lived Californian circuits of Torrey Pines and Pebble Beach were in use, and in 1957 Lime Rock, Connecticut, and Riverside, way out in the Californian desert, began careers which continue today.

Alec Ulmann of Sebring brought modern Formula 1 racing to the USA in 1959, and organised a second World Championship round at Riverside in 1960. Both lost money but after 1961 the event was established at Watkins Glen. In 1976, the US Grand Prix (West) began around the streets of Long Beach, California, and after teething troubles now looks well-established.

Political problems between the various US organising bodies hampered road racing development, such as it was. When the American Automobile Association abolished its Contest Board in 1955 (largely because it panicked after the Le Mans disaster had claimed over eighty dead), it had been sanctioning US motor racing for fifty-three years. From 1902 to 1908, its National Championship was awarded by a press committee, and in 1909 a points system was introduced. The Championship reached a peak in the heady board track days and in the 1930s dwindled to include the Indy '500' and perhaps two or three 100-miler dirt track events. After 1946, the Championship Trail as it was known continued to include many dirt events together with Indianapolis, until 1954 when the Milwaukee track was surfaced. Other tracks were quick to follow suit, like Langhorne and Trenton, and the dirt rounds began to disappear.

The United States Auto Club had been formed to fill the void left by AAA's abdication late in 1955, and under their sanction, track racing of all kinds flourished. By 1968, road races were included (briefly) in the Championship Trail which had grown to accommodate twenty-four events, and by 1971 road races and dirt-track events were separated to form three divisions with the National Championship decided entirely on paved ovals.

Meanwhile, sports car racing had become almost exclusively SCCA's, after a USAC venture into the class had convinced the more conservative organisation that it had better develop its own professional programme. Until that time its progress had been restricted by an insistence on the award of trophies rather than cash for race success. The commercial-minded USAC system was wholely professional. Until 1969, when an SCCA splinter group formed the grandly-named International Motor Sports Association (IMSA), the club had road racing in America to itself.

The spirit of CanAm sports-car racing, with two of the 1972 McLaren-Chevrolets whose predecessors dominated the Championship from 1968–1971. Here drivers are Denny Hulme and Peter Revson at Watkins Glen.

A professional West Coast series of sports car races each autumn gained importance during the 1960s until 1966 when the Canadian–American Challenge Cup sports car Championship was launched with rich sponsorship. British-built Lola cars won that year with John Surtees driving, and from 1967 to 1971 the McLaren team dominated the competition. Then Porsche appeared with turbocharged cars which swept all before them, and when they backed-out, Shadow were left to win a feeble CanAm finale before it died. In 1977, it was revived for Formula 5000-based single-seater cars after their own series had flared briefly and died away. IMSA, meanwhile, attracted a range of international support with a production saloon and GT car series notable for its domination by Porsche and BMW.

All this time, USAC events were drawing in the crowds to watch all manner of track races. Their track directory lists over eighty venues ranging from quarter-mile dirt ovals to 2½-mile speedways like those at Indy, Ontario (California) and Pocono, Pennsylvania. USAC-sanctioned races – all on a national level and therefore independent of FIA regulations – include the high-powered National Championship single-seater cars as used at Indianapolis. Their Dirt Track Championship division is a separate entity these days, contested by classically-styled front-engined single-seater racing cars competing in dirt track races up to 100 miles in length. A Sprint Car division caters for broadly similar machines carrying much less fuel and contesting – as the name implies – shorter dirt track races. At the foot of the USAC national single-seater divisions are the small-engined midget cars, which also race on dirt and with their large starting grids, even performance and rough-and-tumble driving form one of the most exciting forms of motor sport for any spectator to see. There are still-smaller racing cars used in the USA, known as three-quarter midgets and tiny buzz-bombs in a quarter-midget class. The Midget Division Champion of 1971 for example, Danny 'Kid' Caruthers who suffered a tragic fatal accident shortly after gaining his crown, was only twenty-one-years old, yet had eighteen years' racing experience behind him as he had started in quarter-midgets at the age of three!

Mario Andretti, perhaps the most versatile driver the racing world has ever seen, has won Indy and the USAC National Championship, has driven all kinds of sports-racing cars at Le Mans, Sebring, Daytona and Monza and has won World Championship Grand Prix events for Ferrari and Lotus. He was brought up in midget racing and still today considers it '. . . the most educational class of racing I ever took part in; racing every night, every day of the week. You learn a lot that way . . .'

Not that USAC are solely single-seater orientated, for they also operate a well-supported stock car (modified production saloon car) division, unlike the biff-bang type stock car racing seen in Britain, Europe and South Africa, for example.

These heavy and very powerful vehicles race over distances up to 500 miles on a mixture of dirt and paved oval tracks, with the accent on those a mile or less in length although the occasional $2\frac{1}{2}$-mile major speedway is used, such as that at Pocono, Pennsylvania. Broadly similar vehicles also compete under USAC sanction in the Pike's Peak Hill-Climb, the classical twelve-mile dirt road event in Colorado.

The main centre of stock car racing in the USA is in the Confederate States of the 'Deep South' – Virginia, the Carolinas and Florida. There the National Association for Stock Car Auto Racing (NASCAR) rules supreme. It was the brainchild of one

The grandstand banking of the Daytona tri-oval speedway in Florida is sensationally spectacular as hefty NASCAR 'stockers' thunder round it at speeds approaching 190 mph. The Daytona 500-Miles is a stock car classic which has a place today in the southern USA traditions.

man, William H. G. 'Bill' France, who began his fight to organise what had formerly been a type of 'outlaw' sedan racing late in 1947. In 1950, NASCAR found a formal venue at Darlington where a banked oval was opened, and quickly enlarged. Dirt tracks were displaced by more and more paved speedways as the years rolled by, and into the 1970s such superb track facilities as Daytona's tri-oval ($2\frac{1}{2}$ miles round), Darlington, Rockingham, Talladega, Atlanta and Charlotte were recognised justifiably as 'SuperSpeedways'. Some venues have bankings as steep as 33 degrees, and a few – like the Texas and Michigan Speedways – host events sanctioned by other organisations.

NASCAR's annual schedule is regularly crowded with around fifty Grand National Championship rounds and under France's regime strict regulations were enforced and continually updated to provide even competition between manufacturers and teams. The result has been extremely high-speed racing with massive modified 'saloon' cars, slow to accelerate but extremely high-geared and very, very fast after a run-up to achieve their maximum speed. Very valuable cash prize funds are provided, and one driver – Richard Petty – had by the early 1970s made himself a dollar millionaire purely from his winnings.

Below NASCAR and USAC level there are literally hundreds of small tracks scattered across the vast expanse of the USA which stage races for outdated modified stock cars, minor-league midget and sprint car events, demolition derbys and even figure-eight races! Myriad small regional clubs and associations provide their organisation but there is little intermingling between the various types of motor sport and rather than there being one logical progression from bush-league to the dizzy heights of Indianapolis-style competition, there are instead a bewildering number of shorter 'ladders', all side by side and many leading nowhere.

Racing Classes

The races sanctioned by the United States Auto Club are the most widely representative of modern American track racing, and primary regulations for the classes they recognise line-up as given below.

National Championship Division – The premier-league of Indy-style track racing, caters for single-seater racing cars powered (until 1st January 1981) by four-stroke overhead cam piston engines of not more than 161·703 cid (2·65 litres) if supercharged; of 274·590 cid (4·5 litres) unsupercharged, or – if based on stock production units with pushrod valve operation – of not more than 209·3 cid (3·43 litres) supercharged and up to 355·136 cid (5·82 litres) unsupercharged.

The wedge-shaped racing car worked particularly well at Indianapolis and on the other USAC ovals and it was developed into winning form by McLaren designer Gordon Coppuck with his M16-family of cars, like this one, driven by Denny Hulme.

Strict regulations govern the size and settings of exhaust-driven turbocharger units, which are used to supercharge the popular 2·65-litre Offenhauser/Drake four-cylinder and V8 engines and the Foyt and Cosworth DFX V8s used in this style of racing. The turbocharger's maximum permissible inlet bore size is restricted to 2·940 inches – remember that restricting the air capable of entering an engine system effectively restricts the power which it can put out. The compressor turbine wheel size is limited to 3·60 inches and the maximum turbine wheel diameter is 3·50 inches. Only one turbocharger is allowed per engine.

All qualification runs have to be made with an approved turbocharger pressure-relief valve installed, passing a maximum manifold pressure of 80 inches of mercury. All such valves are set and calibrated by the USAC Technical Committee.

Car size is restricted to within 15 feet overall length, 80 inches overall width, they must have a wheelbase of at least 96 inches and track must be at least 47 inches. Overall weight, less fuel, oil, water and driver, must exceed 1,500 lb with supercharged engines, or 1,425 lb unsupercharged. Ballast may not be added to satisfy this requirement, i.e. weight must be built-in safety.

Strict limitations are applied to the car's construction and the height, width and positioning of aerodynamic aids. No airfoil may extend more than 42 inches behind the centre lines of the rear wheels, for example, while the maximum width of the rear airfoil (which must be centred between the rear wheels – significant in these left-turn only, asymmetrically set-up cars) is set at 43 inches.

Wheel limitations allow only four to be used – stipulated as two at the front and two at the rear (!) – and their rim diameter has to be at least 15 inches. Rim width for undriven wheels is limited to a maximum of 10 inches while rim width for driven wheels has a maximum of 14 inches.

Strict fuel load regulations were enforced after the fiery Indianapolis '500' of 1973 and the adverse impact it had on the nation's media attitude to USAC-style racing.

The maximum capacity of the car's fuel system must not exceed 40 US gallons and for some years this had to be concentrated on the vehicle's left-hand side – away from the crash barrier side. In 1976 a new Crashworthy Fuel System became available, allowing up to 20 gallons to be carried on the car's right-hand side once more. Fuel is restricted to methanol only and partly to restrict engine tune a strict limitation is placed upon the amount of fuel any one team may provide for their car in any event. This limitation is based on a fuel consumption of 1·8 miles per US gallon, fed into the car through a single hose from a gravity-feed tower tank not more than 84 inches high.

Four-wheel drive is banned, although either front or rear-wheel drive may be used, and safety regulations fill several pages of the USAC Official Competition Rules book. Indy developed roll-over and crash-bars, accelerator pedal toe-straps to allow a driver to pull closed a sticking throttle, safety harnesses and other items which found their way into Grand Prix racing many years later. What gives USAC racing a special character is the old-established tradition of naming the cars. Thus instead of the 'McLaren–Offenhauser' style designation which might be used in Europe, describing chassis constructor-engine constructor, we find such exotics as the 'SugaRipe Prune Juice Special' and the 'Indianapolis on a Shoestring Special'. All names have to be cleared by a USAC committee, and lurking in the background is an all-pervasive regulation stating that 'Cars and crews whose appearance detract from the character of the program, shall be excluded'.

Championship Dirt Car Division – The USAC Dirt Championship is contested mainly by front-engined single-seaters looking very much like the traditional Indy roadsters of yore. They are upright and antiquated-looking by European standards but the racing is enormously fast and exciting, and spectators have the added attraction of being able to see the driver at work, exposed in his roll-over cage protected cockpit.

Engines are limited to 280·692 cid (4·6 litres) maximum capacity unsupercharged if they have overhead camshaft valve operation, with an allowance of 332·999 cid (5·457 litres) for stock-block, pushrod-valve units.

Wheel limitations are as for the National Championship cars, as are drive requirements. Overall length of the complete car is limited to 15 feet, overall width 80 inches, wheelbase a minimum of 96 inches and track at least 47 inches. Minimum empty weight is 1,425 lb, ballast not permitted. Fuel allowance on board the car is no less than 75 US gallons, and there are myriad extra regulations governing construction, engine development and safety.

Interestingly, there are engine options limiting 'special rocker-arm single non-overhead camshaft non-supercharged engines' to 305·1 cid (5 litres); two-stroke engines, other than diesels, are acceptable if limited to a maximum of 170·856 cid (2·8 litres); unsupercharged diesels carry a 305·1 cid (5 litre) limit and gas turbine engines are limited to a maximum total annulus area at the entrance to the first moving compressor stage of 11·999 square inches. This is the limitation which destroyed turbocar prospects in the National Championship speedway events. Finally, rotating (Wankel-type) combustion engines, unsupercharged, are admissible to a maximum displacement of 256·284 cid (4·2 litres) – that figure being judged on the maximum volume of one working chamber, minus that same chamber's minimum volume, multiplied by two – multiplied by the number of rotors . . . still with me?

In 1977, the Dirt Championship was very firecely-disputed, with 33 drivers sharing in the 48 points-scoring finish positions available from the four qualifying races. These were all on one-mile fairgrounds tracks, covering 100 miles each at Springfield, DuQuoin, Indianapolis and Syracuse.

Sprint Car Division – This class caters generally for small-scale versions of the big Championship dirt cars, designed to run on both paved and dirt tracks, usually of around half-mile lap length.

Engine regulations impose maximum limitations of 305·1 cid (5 litres) on unsupercharged stock production pushrod engines, while other units have to be submitted to and approved by the Division directors before being accepted for competition.

Vehicle dimensions are limited to a wheelbase of no less than 84 inches and no more than 90 inches; minimum track of 47 inches;

overall width no more than 78 inches, and overall length not more than 14 feet.

The cars must be of the open-wheel, open cockpit type, with the cockpit opening between engine bay and rear axle, no airfoil aids, and with similar wheel and drive restrictions to those for National Championship machines. Minimum empty weight is 1,400 lb. Roll-over cages, 'nerf' protective bars at front and rear and angled in front of the rear wheels are all mandatory and there is a mass of other safety requirements.

The USAC Sprint Car Division has always been the scene of stiff competition. In 1977, there were no less than 44 sanctioned events, offering prize money of $473,439! Run mainly on half-mile and five-eighths-mile tracks, always with very large starting fields the Sprints are a major crowd-pleasing form of American-style motor racing.

Midget Car Division – Catering for still-smaller front-engined open-wheel, open-cockpit racing cars, the Midget Car regulations demand a minimum wheelbase of 66 inches and a maximum wheelbase of 76 inches. There are no other dimensional restraints upon the general concept of the car, though as with the Sprint vehicles airfoil aids are banned and the cockpit opening must be located directly behind the engine compartment. Wheel regulations demand the use of either 12-inch or 13-inch diameter rims, limited to 8 inches in width, carrying tyres no more than 12 inches wide when measured side-wall to side-wall. Four-wheel drive is banned, front or rear wheels may be driven.

Engine limitations are all-embracing, and complex: four-stroke, twin overhead camshaft four-cylinder, water-cooled engines are restricted to a maximum of 127 cid, allowing Offenhauser–Drake, Chevrolet Cosworth Vega, Rassey, Jensen-Healey and Cosworth-Ford engines to compete.

Twin overhead camshaft, air-cooled engines are limited to no more than 109·000 cid – admitting the Porsche Spyder four-cylinder 547/5A power unit.

Modified stock production pushrod rocker arm non-OHC engines using another type two-valve cylinder head are limited to a maximum of 157·000 cid – admitting the four-cylinder, in-line Chevrolet Sesco, Ford Sesco, Chevrolet II, Chevrolet V4 (literally a V8 chopped in two), Daimler V8 and Buick V6.

Modified stock engines as above using a four-valve cylinder head are allowed 148·000 cid – approved power units including the four-cylinder inline Sesco Chevrolet and Sesco-Ford with Weslake head.

Stock production engines with single overhead camshaft valve operation and two-valve per cylinder head are limited to 143·000 cid – admitting six-cylinder Ford Falcon, and four-cylinder Ford Pinto, Chevvy Vega and Dodge Colt units.

Stock production air-cooled, two-valves are allowed a maximum of 140·000 cid – admitting four-cylinder VW, Porsche, Corvair and the air-cooled SCAT engine.

Stock production air-cooled units with single OHC valve actuation are limited to 135·000 cid – admitting Porsche 911 six-cylinder 'flat' engines.

Special racing single cam, pushrod four-valve head engines are restricted to below 135·000 cid – admitting the very special Sesco modular quadrasphere power unit.

Racing engines with two-valve heads using one non-overhead camshaft for each side are limited to no more than 148·000 cid – admitting Sesco 2X4 and SCAT water-cooled units.

Single OHC four-valve head engines are allowed 125·000 cid – admitting the Porsche 911.

Turbocharged and supercharged engines are positively banned.

The effect of this mass of regulations and conditions is to provide fairly even competition throughout the Midget car field, and the racing is fierce to an almost white-hot intensity! In 1977 the Volkswagen engines won 32 of the season's 48 races, while the others fell to a combination of Chevy II, Sesco 2X4, the Cosworth Vega and the Pinto. Circuits used are predominantly paved, the longest track being the five-eighth-miler at Clermont, Indiana, while the shortest are only one-tenth-milers as at Fort Wayne, Indianapolis, Louisville and Norfolk.

Stock Car Division – While in Europe, South Africa and other parts of the world 'stock car' suggests a battered demolition derby-style saloon, in the USA the term derives simply from 'stock production' – what in Europe might be termed a touring car.

USAC stock cars are derived from US manufactured models of the current year and previous three years, limited to hard top, two- or four-door sedans designed to carry four or more passengers. The regulations specifically ban roadsters, Jeeps, sports cars, taxis, station wagons and trucks! The car must be marketed through regular channels and must in any case be approved for competition by the Club's committees.

Engines must be normal internal-combustion piston type running on automotive gasoline, normally aspirated and with modifications allowed only within basic limitations. Engine capacity shall not exceed 355·000 cid beginning with the 1980 season, while formerly they have been allowed to reach 429·999 cid.

Dimensional limitations demand that the stock car's wheelbase shall be within a half-inch of the original manufactured dimension. Vehicle weight, including fuel, oil and water but not driver must be a minimum of 3,300 lb for cars of 108-inch wheelbase and above and a 355 cid engine. Cars with a 113-inch wheelbase and above and engines of between 355 and 429 cid shall weigh a minimum of 3,700 lb.

Ground clearance must be at least 4½ inches, and one side of the car must not be more than 2 inches higher than the other – again to limit assymetrical setting-up to produce a freak track car. Similarly the distance from the front centre-line of the crankshaft to the ground must not be less than 10 inches. A mass of safety and specification regulations are appended to produce a family of very fast yet extremely robust sedan-bodied track racers.

During 1977, the USAC Stock Championship included a round on the superspeedway at Ontario, California, where A. J. Foyt qualified his SuperSpeedway at College Station, Texas, where Ron Hutcherson qualified his Plymouth Volare at a staggering 168·303 mph, to the Indiana State Fairgrounds dirt track where Ramo Stott's winning Plymouth had qualified at 93·506 mph. Race distances varied from 100 miles on the dirt to 500 miles at College Station – a rich and varied form of very serious motor sport.

Mini-Indy Division – A relative newcomer to the USAC ranks, demanding single-seat open-wheeler racing cars based on Volkswagen original components, like Formula SuperVee. Car design and body fitting is fairly free, wheelbase and track dimensions are unrestricted, but there is a minimum weight limit of 882 lb for air-cooled engined cars and of 928 lb (as qualified or raced, but without driver) for water-cooled. Only two front and two rear wheels are allowed, with 13-inch diameter rims, 6 inches wide at the front and 8 inches at the rear. No more than four forward speeds may be provided in the Volkswagen-cased transmission.

This division made its début in 1977 as a very sensible move to provide a foot-of-the-ladder training ground for future National Championship car drivers. Formerly, the change from front-engined midget, dirt and sprint car to mid-engined, sophisticated Championship racer has been a shock to many aspiring drivers. A race distance of 100 km was decided upon, and the races were run on the Championship Trail speedways as supporting events for major-league rounds.

At Trenton, New Jersey, the SuperVees averaged 117·176 mph for their 100 km, where the 150-mile record stands to Bobby Unser's 1974 Eagle at 155·799 mph. Still, Mini-Indy is a logical start – a long-awaited launching pad for aspiring mid-engined, single-seater aerodynamically aided speedway racers.

8 Racing the World Over

While motor racing at its major level is organised in the countries of Europe by the sporting commission of the FIA, and US motor sports are conducted as already described by that huge nation's diverse authorities, the sport of circuit racing is well-established elsewhere in the world, on both sides of the so-called Iron Curtain and deep into the Southern Hemisphere. One Communist-bloc country, Czechoslovakia, has an integral round in the European Touring Car Championship and several eastern European nations contest the annual Peace (or Friendship) Cup series of minor-formula single-seater races. East Germany, Hungary, Poland and the USSR have all supported a Formula 3-style class using cars based on home production car parts, and they make use of horse-race tracks, stadia and frozen lakes in addition to less restrictive – and often quite hair-raising – closed public road courses.

Canada

In Canada, motor racing has been well-established for many years, although on nothing like such a diverse scale as in the neighbouring USA. Road circuits like Mosport Park, Ste Jovite and Edmonton have all been established on private land, and have hosted International CanAm Championship, Formula 5000, Formula Atlantic and (in the case of the first two) the International Formula 1 Grand Prix race. Formula Atlantic is well-established today as the major Canadian single-seater class, and rounds in the Championship are run on such closed public road circuits as the remarkably tight and daunting round-the-houses affair at Les Trois Rivières.

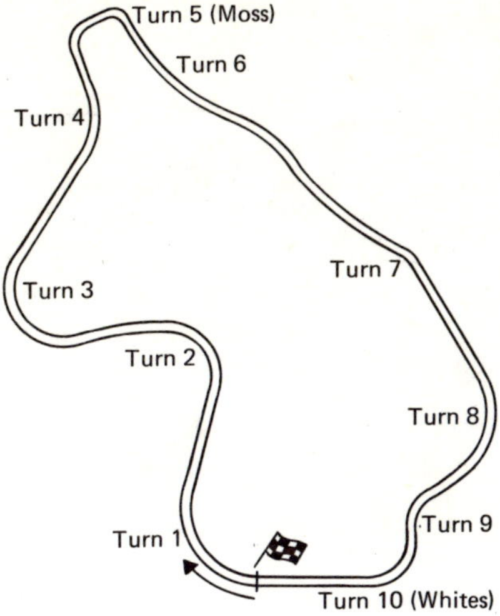

Mosport Park, Canada.

South America

In South America, the nations of Argentina and Brazil have led the way, with a motor racing history going back to the dawn of motoring itself and having produced such drivers as the legendary Juan-Manuel Fangio (five times World Champion), Froilan Gonzalez, Emerson Fittipaldi (twice Champion), Carlos

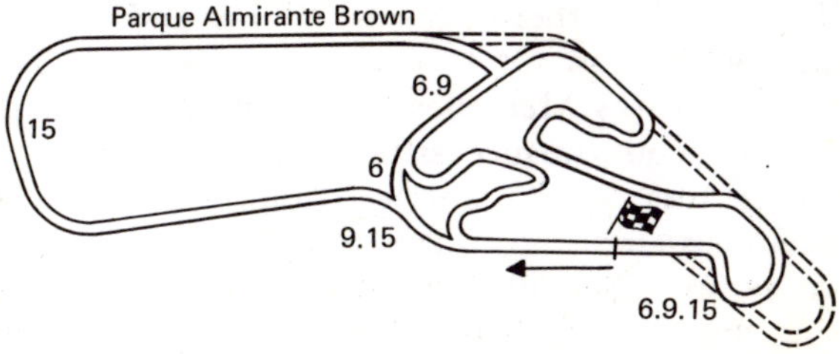

Buenos Aires, Argentina.

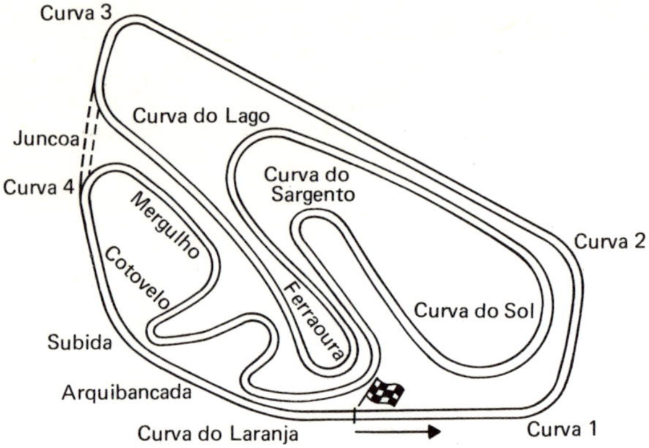

Interlagos, Brazil.

Reutemann and the late Carlos Pace. Before World War II International Grand Prix class racing took place on the incredible Gavea circuit (known as 'The Devil's Springboard') around the Sugar Loaf mountain at Rio de Janeiro in Brazil, while the Argentinians, Peruvians and Chileans indulged in cross-country production car *Carretera* racing over distances up to 6,000 miles! Fangio was brought up in just such a class, and on a lesser level many closed public road circuit and track-race events were also organised. Immediately postwar, international racing was heavily promoted by the Peron Government of Argentina, and such stars as Wimille (who died there), Varzi, Farina and Villoresi journeyed south of the equator to compete with their Grand Prix machinery. The works Mercedes-Benz team made their postwar Grand Prix car début, unsuccessfully, in Argentina in 1951, and often those on this South American tour took in races at São Paulo's Interlagos circuit in Brazil. In the 1960s, the Argentinian *Temporada* series – so-called because of the midsummer heat there during the northern hemisphere's winter – was revived for Formula 2 cars and a great South American revival began which put such drivers as Fittipaldi, Reutemann and Pace into top-class Formula 1 racing.

Today, South American racing majors on local touring car and GT Formulae, Formula Vee and Formula 'SudAm' single-seaters built around production components, and there are also national variations on the Formula 1 and Formula 2 themes.

South Africa

Still in the southern hemisphere, South Africa has a strong motor racing tradition; prewar the Auto Union team raced in the country just as they did on the Gavea at Rio de Janeiro. For many years a national Formula 1 series kept alive many obsolete Grand

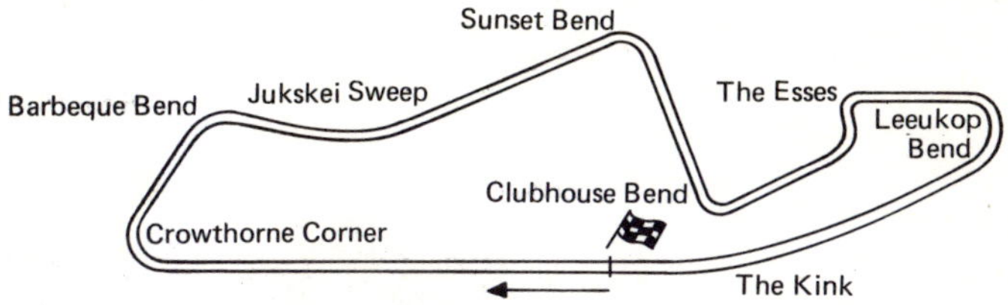

Kylami, South Africa.

Prix cars sold off by the World Championship teams, but today this has been re-graded as an Atlantic series and the F1s are laid-up or in museums. A 'Springbok Championship' for sports cars also formed an entertaining mid-South African summer series for visiting Europeans, but this has now died as has the class itself (virtually) at international level.

Australasia

In Australia and New Zealand, the motor racing tradition is even more deeply ingrained, and these nations have given us World

Champion racing drivers like Jack Brabham, Denny Hulme and Bruce McLaren, who between them built and drove racing cars which have innumerable race wins, seven Formula 1 World Championships, five CanAm Championships and many other titles – including three Indianapolis '500' track classic victories – to their names!

Racing in Australia began on circuits like Phillip Island, the Maroubra Speedbowl, the Melbourne Motordrome and Bathurst prewar, and grew in stature during the 1950s and early 1960s. In 1964, the Tasman Championship was introduced, during the northern hemisphere's winter, and with qualifying rounds in New Zealand and Australia it was contested by Brabham, McLaren,

Racing in Australia reached its height during the 1960s when all the leading GP drivers wintered there for the Tasman Championship series of races which the Continent shared with New Zealand. Here at Warwick Farm, Sydney, Jack Brabham leads the bunch, 1967.

Jim Clark and Lotus, Graham Hill and Jackie Stewart with BRM, and by many other notables. The cars were virtually Formula 1 standard in disguise, and then as the series lost support into the 1970s, it was downgraded to Formula 5000 and today lives in relative obscurity open to Formula Atlantic vehicles. Even so, the influence particularly of New Zealand and New Zealanders on world-class motor racing has been immense, and that such a small population can throw up so many immensely talented drivers, designers and racing administrators is a commentary upon 'Kiwi' enthusiasm.

The Far East

Formula Atlantic, in a modified form, is also the staple single-seater racing diet of the Far Eastern nations, where circuits are used regularly in Malaysia, Singapore and the Portuguese enclave of Macao on the coast of mainland China. Racing in Japan is more highly formalised and better developed, with some fine racing circuits on private ground staging races for all manner of touring cars, national single-seater Formulae and classes corresponding with international 2-litre sports and Formula 2.

★ ★ ★

Motor racing now seems ready to take hold and flourish in some oil-rich countries of the Middle East and although it has seen more healthy times than the mid-1970s, its general growth continues.

The Land Speed Record

Many people confuse the concept of the struggle to be 'fastest on land' with motor racing as a sport, but in general terms the two activities are worlds apart. When the Count de Chasseloup-Laubat set the first officially-timed record at 39·24 mph in 1898 in his Jeantaud electric car, this was not an accurate reflection of the ultimate pace of which horseless carriages of the period were capable. It was simply the fastest which had ever been timed. From the beginning a degree of specialisation had crept into LSR cars, and after 1926 when the last dual-purpose LSR/road racing car had some success, the record breakers became such highly-specialised projectiles as Sir Malcolm Campbell's *Bluebirds*, Segrave's Sunbeam *Slug* and *Golden Arrow*, and the beautiful though ill-fated Stutz *Black Hawk*. The essence of all these machines was that their power was transmitted to the straight-line course through their wheels. Finding courses long enough and smooth enough was a great problem. Seaside beaches as at Pendine in Britain and Daytona-Ormond Beach in Florida (even Nine-Mile beach in New Zealand) were outgrown, and finally the record breakers took to the vast expanse of dried salt lakes as at Bonneville, Utah, USA. During the 1960s, low-budget American hot-rodders began outstripping wheel-driven speeds with streamlined jet and rocket-powered vehicles, and today the FIA recognises two speed classes, one for wheel-driven and one for reaction-driven cars. The list of records established is as follows:

WORLD LAND SPEED RECORD 1898–1970

Year	*Driver (Vehicle)*	*Location*	*Speed*
1898	Chasseloup-Laubat (Jeantaud)	Acheres	63·14 kph (39·24 mph)
1899	Jenatzy (Jenatzy)	Acheres	66·64 kph (41·42 mph)
1899	Chasseloup-Laubat (Jeantaud)	Acheres	70·29 kph (43·69 mph)
1899	Jenatzy (Jenatzy)	Acheres	80·32 kph (49·92 mph)
1899	Chasseloup-Laubat (Jeantaud)	Acheres	92·68 kph (57·60 mph)
1899	Jenatzy (Jenatzy)	Acheres	105·86 kph (65·79 mph)
1902	Serpollet (Serpollet)	Nice	120·77 kph (75·06 mph)
1902	Vanderbilt (Mors)	Ablis	122·41 kph (76·08 mph)
1902	Fournier (Mors)	Dourdan	123·25 kph (76·60 mph)
1902	Augieres (Mors)	Dourdan	124·10 kph (77·13 mph)
1903	Duray (Gobron-Brillié)	Ostend	134·30 kph (83·47 mph)
1903	Duray (Gobron-Brillié)	Dourdan	136·33 kph (84·73 mph)
*1904	Ford (Ford)	Lake St Clair	147·01 kph (91·37 mph)
*1904	Vanderbilt (Mercedes)	Daytona	148·51 kph (92·30 mph)
1904	Rigolly (Gobron-Brillie)	Nice	152·50 kph (94·78 mph)
1904	de Caters (Mercedes)	Ostend	156·48 kph (97·25 mph)
1904	Rigolly (Gobron-Brillié)	Ostend	166·61 kph (103·55 mph)
1904	Baras (Darracq)	Ostend	168·17 kph (104·52 mph)
*1905	Macdonald (Napier)	Daytona	168·38 kph (104·65 mph)
1905	Hemery (Darracq)	Arles-Salon	176·43 kph (109·65 mph)
1906	Marriott (Stanley)	Daytona	195·61 kph (121·57 mph)
1909	Hemery (Benz)	Brooklands	202·65 kph (125·95 mph)

Year	*Driver (Vehicle)*	*Location*	*Speed*
*1910	Oldfield (Benz)	Daytona	211·22 kph (131·28 mph)
*1911	Burman (Benz)	Daytona	227·46 kph (141·37 mph)
1914	Hornsted (Benz)	Brooklands	199·68 kph (124·10 mph) (two-way average)
*1919	de Palma (Packard)	Daytona	241·15 kph (149·875 mph)
*1920	Milton (Duesenberg)	Daytona	251·05 kph (156·03 mph)
1922	Guinness (Sunbeam)	Brooklands	215·20 kph (133·75 mph)
1924	Thomas (Delage)	Arpajon	230·59 kph (143·31 mph)
1924	Eldridge (Fiat)	Arpajon	234·93 kph (146·01 mph)
1925	Campbell (*Bluebird*)	Pendine	235·17 kph (146·16 mph)
1925	Campbell (*Bluebird*)	Pendine	242·57 kph (150·76 mph)
1926	Segrave (Sunbeam)	Southport	245·09 kph (152·33 mph)
1926	Thomas (Thomas)	Pendine	272·40 kph (169·30 mph)
1926	Thomas (Thomas)	Pendine	275·17 kph (171·02 mph)
1927	Campbell (*Bluebird*)	Pendine	281·39 kph (174·883 mph)
1927	Segrave (Sunbeam)	Daytona	327·90 kph (203·792 mph)
1928	Campbell (*Bluebird*)	Daytona	332·99 kph (206·956 mph)
1928	Keech (White)	Daytona	333·95 kph (207·552 mph)
1929	Segrave (Irving *Golden Arrow*)	Daytona	372·39 kph (231·446 mph)
1931	Campbell (*Bluebird*)	Daytona	395·96 kph (246·09 mph)
1932	Campbell (*Bluebird*)	Daytona	408·64 kph (253·97 mph)
1933	Campbell (*Bluebird*)	Daytona	438·39 kph (272·46 mph)
1935	Campbell (*Bluebird*)	Daytona	445·40 kph (276·82 mph)
1935	Campbell (*Bluebird*)	Bonneville	484·52 kph (301·129 mph)
1937	Eyston (*Thunderbolt*)	Bonneville	502·00 kph (312·00 mph)
1938	Eyston (*Thunderbolt*)	Bonneville	555·91 kph (345·50 mph)
1938	Cobb (*Railton Mobil Special*)	Bonneville	563·47 kph (350·20 mph)
1938	Eyston (*Thunderbolt*)	Bonneville	575·22 kph (357·50 mph)
1939	Cobb (*Railton Mobil Special*)	Bonneville	594·85 kph (369·70 mph)
1947	Cobb (*Railton Mobil Special*)	Bonneville	634·27 kph (394·20 mph)
*1963	Breedlove (Breedlove)	Bonneville	655·59 kph (407·45 mph)
1964	D. Campbell (*Bluebird*)	Lake Eyre	648·59 kph (403·10 mph)
1964	Green (*Wingfoot Express*)	Bonneville	664·84 kph (413·20 mph)
1964	Arfons (*Green Monster*)	Bonneville	698·34 kph (434·02 mph)
1964	Breedlove (Breedlove)	Bonneville	754·17 kph (468·72 mph)
1964	Breedlove (Breedlove)	Bonneville	846·78 kph (526·28 mph)
1964	Arfons (*Green Monster*)	Bonneville	863·57 kph (536·71 mph)
1965	Breedlove (Breedlove)	Bonneville	893·77 kph (555·483 mph)
1965	Arfons (*Green Monster*)	Bonneville	927·67 kph (576·553 mph)
1965	Summers (Summers *Goldenrod*)	Bonneville	658·53 kph (409·277 mph) wheel-driven record*
1965	Breedlove (Breedlove)	Bonneville	966·37 kph (600·601 mph)
1970	Gabelich (*Blue Flame*)	Bonneville	1014·29 kph (630·388 mph)

* Indicates record not ratified by the FIA, the international governing body, who ratify the record in kph. All other speeds in Appendix I are given in mph only.

Appendix 1
Championship Statistics

THE DRIVERS' WORLD CHAMPIONSHIP 1950–77

Year	*Driver*	*Nationality*	*Car*	*Points*
1950	Dr Giuseppe 'Nino' Farina	(I)	Alfa Romeo	30
	Juan-Manuel Fangio	(ARG)	Alfa Romeo	27
1951	Juan-Manuel Fangio	(ARG)	Alfa Romeo	31
	Alberto Ascari	(I)	Ferrari	25
1952	Alberto Ascari	(I)	Ferrari	36
	Dr Giuseppe 'Nino' Farina	(I)	Ferrari	25
1953	Alberto Ascari	(I)	Ferrari	$34\frac{1}{2}$
	Juan-Manuel Fangio	(ARG)	Maserati	28
1954	Juan-Manuel Fangio	(ARG)	Maserati and Mercedes-Benz	42
	Froilan Gonzalez	(ARG)	Ferrari	$25\frac{1}{7}$
1955	Juan-Manuel Fangio	(ARG)	Mercedes-Benz	40
	Stirling Moss	(GB)	Mercedes-Benz	27
1956	Juan-Manuel Fangio	(ARG)	Ferrari	30
	Stirling Moss	(GB)	Maserati	27
1957	Juan-Manuel Fangio	(ARG)	Maserati	40
	Stirling Moss	(GB)	Vanwall	25
1958	Mike Hawthorn	(GB)	Ferrari	42
	Stirling Moss	(GB)	Vanwall and Cooper-Climax	41
1959	Jack Brabham	(AUS)	Cooper-Climax	31
	Tony Brooks	(GB)	Ferrari	27
1960	Jack Brabham	(AUS)	Cooper-Climax	43
	Bruce McLaren	(NZ)	Cooper-Climax	34
1961	Phil Hill	(USA)	Ferrari	34
	*Wolfgang von Trips	(D)	Ferrari	33

Year	*Driver*	*Nationality*	*Car*	*Points*
1962	Graham Hill	(GB)	BRM	42
	Jim Clark	(GB)	Lotus-Climax	30
1963	Jim Clark	(GB)	Lotus-Climax	54
	Graham Hill	(GB)	BRM	29
1964	John Surtees	(GB)	Ferrari	40
	Graham Hill	(GB)	BRM	39
1965	Jim Clark	(GB)	Lotus-Climax	54
	Graham Hill	(GB)	BRM	40
1966	Jack Brabham	(AUS)	Brabham-Repco	42
	John Surtees	(GB)	Ferrari and Cooper-Maserati	28
1967	Denny Hulme	(NZ)	Brabham-Repco	51
	Jack Brabham	(AUS)	Brabham-Repco	46
1968	Graham Hill	(GB)	Lotus-Ford	48
	Jackie Stewart	(GB)	Matra-Ford	36
1969	Jackie Stewart	(GB)	Matra-Ford	63
	Jacky Ickx	(B)	Brabham-Ford	37
1970	*Jochen Rindt	(A)	Lotus-Ford	45
	Jacky Ickx	(B)	Ferrari	40
1971	Jackie Stewart	(GB)	Tyrrell-Ford	62
	Ronnie Peterson	(S)	March-Ford	33
1972	Emerson Fittipaldi	(BRA)	Lotus-Ford	61
	Jackie Stewart	(GB)	Tyrrell-Ford	45
1973	Jackie Stewart	(GB)	Tyrrell-Ford	71
	Emerson Fittipaldi	(BRA)	Lotus-Ford	55
1974	Emerson Fittipaldi	(BRA)	McLaren-Ford	55
	Clay Regazzoni	(CH)	Ferrari	52
1975	Niki Lauda	(A)	Ferrari	64½
	Emerson Fittipaldi	(BRA)	McLaren-Ford	45
1976	James Hunt	(GB)	McLaren-Ford	69
	Niki Lauda	(A)	Ferrari	68
1977	Niki Lauda	(A)	Ferrari	72
	Jody Scheckter	(ZA)	Wolf-Ford	55

* Killed during the season

FRENCH GRAND PRIX

Year	*Circuit*	*Driver(s)*	Car	*Average* speed
1906	Le Mans	Ferenc Szisz	Renault	62·9 mph
1907	Dieppe	Felice Nazzaro	Fiat	70·5 mph
1908	Dieppe	Christian Lautenschlager	Mercedes	69·0 mph
1912	Dieppe	Georges Boillot	Peugeot	68·4 mph
1913	Amiens	Georges Boillot	Peugeot	71·6 mph
1914	Lyon	Christian Lautenschlager	Mercedes	65·3 mph
1921	Le Mans	Jimmy Murphy	Duesenberg	78·1 mph
1922	Strasbourg	Felice Nazzaro	Fiat	79·2 mph
1923	Tours	Henry Segrave	Sunbeam	75·3 mph
1924	Lyon	Giuseppe Campari	Alfa Romeo	71·0 mph
1925	Montlhéry	Robert Benoist and Albert Divo	Delage	69·7 mph
1926	Miramas	Jules Goux	Bugatti	68·2 mph
1927	Montlhéry	Robert Benoist	Delage	77·2 mph
1928	*Comminges	'Williams'	Bugatti	66·4 mph
1929	Le Mans	'Williams'	Bugatti	82·7 mph
1930	Pau	Phillippe Etancelin	Bugatti	90·4 mph
1931	Montlhéry	Louis Chiron and Achille Varzi	Bugatti	78·7 mph
1932	Reims	Tazio Nuvolari	Alfa Romeo	92·3 mph
1933	Montlhéry	Giuseppe Campari	Maserati	81·5 mph
1934	Montlhéry	Louis Chrion	Alfa Romeo	85·1 mph
1935	Montlhéry	Rudolf Caracciola	Mercedes-Benz	77·42 mph
1936	*Montlhéry	Jean-Pierre Wimille and Raymond Sommer	Bugatti	77·9 mph
1937	*Montlhéry	Louis Chiron	Talbot	82·5 mph
1938	Reims	Manfred von Brauchitsch	Mercedes-Benz	101·1 mph
1939	Reims	H. P. Muller	Auto Union	105·3 mph
1947	Lyon-Parilly	Louis Chiron	Talbot-Lago	78·1 mph
1948	Reims	Jean-Pierre Wimille	Alfa Romeo	102·9 mph
1949	*Comminges	Charles Pozzi	Delahaye	87·9 mph
1950	Reims	Juan-Manuel Fangio	Alfa Romeo	104·9 mph
1951	Reims	Juan-Manuel Fangio and Luigi Fagioli	Alfa Romeo	110·9 mph
1952	Rouen	Alberto Ascari	Ferrari	80·1 mph
1953	Reims	Mike Hawthorn	Ferrari	113·7 mph
1954	Reims	Juan-Manuel Fangio	Mercedes-Benz	115·7 mph
1956	Reims	Peter Collins	Ferrari	122·2 mph
1957	Rouen	Juan-Manuel Fangio	Maserati	100·0 mph
1958	Reims	Mike Hawthorn	Ferrari	125·5 mph
1959	Reims	Tony Brooks	Ferrari	127·4 mph
1960	Reims	Jack Brabham	Cooper-Climax	131·9 mph
1961	Reims	Giancàrlo Baghetti	Ferrari	119·8 mph
1962	Rouen	Dan Gurney	Porsche	101·9 mph
1963	Reims	Jim Clark	Lotus-Climax	125·3 mph
1964	Rouen	Dan Gurney	Brabham-Climax	108·8 mph
1965	Clermont	Jim Clark	Lotus-Climax	89·2 mph
1966	Reims	Jack Brabham	Brabham-Repco	136·9 mph
1967	Le Mans	Jack Brabham	Brabham-Repco	98·9 mph
1968	Rouen	Jacky Ickx	Ferrari	100·4 mph
1969	Clermont	Jackie Stewart	Matra-Ford	97·7 mph
1970	Clermont	Jochen Rindt	Lotus-Ford	98·4 mph
1971	Ricard	Jackie Stewart	Tyrrell-Ford	111·6 mph
1972	Clermont	Jackie Stewart	Tyrrell-Ford	101·6 mph
1973	Ricard	Ronnie Peterson	Lotus-Ford	115·2 mph

Year	Circuit	Driver(s)	Car	Average speed
1974	Dijon	Ronnie Peterson	Lotus-Ford	119·7 mph
1975	Ricard	Niki Lauda	Ferrari	116·6 mph
1976	Ricard	James Hunt	McLaren-Ford	115·8 mph
1977	Dijon	Mario Andretti	Lotus-Ford	113·7 mph
1978	Ricard	Mario Andretti	Lotus-Ford	118·3 mph

* Sports car races

BRITISH GRAND PRIX

Year	Circuit	Driver(s)	Car	Average speed
1926	Brooklands	Robert Senechal and Louis Wagner	Delage	71·6 mph
1927	Brooklands	Robert Benoist	Delage	85·6 mph
1935	Donington	Richard Shuttleworth	Alfa Romeo	63·9 mph
1936	Donington	Dick Seaman and Hans Ruesch	Alfa Romeo	69·2 mph
1937	Donington	Bernd Rosemeyer	Auto Union	82·9 mph
1938	Donington	Tazio Nuvolari	Auto Union	80·4 mph
1949	Silverstone	Tulo de Graffenried	Maserati	77·3 mph
1950	Silverstone	Giuseppe Farina	Alfa Romeo	90·0 mph
1951	Silverstone	Froilan Gonzalez	Ferrari	96·1 mph
1952	Silverstone	Alberto Ascari	Ferrari	90·9 mph
1953	Silverstone	Alberto Ascari	Ferrari	92·9 mph
1954	Silverstone	Froilan Gonzalez	Ferrari	89·6 mph
1955	Aintree	Stirling Moss	Mercedes-Benz	86·4 mph
1956	Silverstone	Juan-Manuel Fangio	Ferrari	98·6 mph
1957	Aintree	Stirling Moss and Tony Brooks	Vanwall	86·8 mph
1958	Silverstone	Peter Collins	Ferrari	102·0 mph
1959	Aintree	Jack Brabham	Cooper-Climax	89·8 mph
1960	Silverstone	Jack Brabham	Cooper-Climax	108·6 mph
1961	Aintree	Wolfgang von Trips	Ferrari	83·9 mph
1962	Aintree	Jim Clark	Lotus-Climax	92·2 mph
1963	Silverstone	Jim Clark	Lotus-Climax	107·7 mph
1964	Brands Hatch	Jim Clark	Lotus-Climax	94·1 mph
1965	Silverstone	Jim Clark	Lotus-Climax	112·0 mph
1966	Brands Hatch	Jack Brabham	Brabham-Repco	95·4 mph
1967	Silverstone	Jim Clark	Lotus-Ford	117·6 mph
1968	Brands Hatch	Jo Siffert	Lotus-Ford	104·8 mph
1969	Silverstone	Jackie Stewart	Matra-Ford	127·2 mph
1970	Brands Hatch	Jochen Rindt	Lotus-Ford	108·6 mph
1971	Silverstone	Jackie Stewart	Tyrrell-Ford	130·5 mph
1972	Brands Hatch	Emerson Fittipaldi	Lotus-Ford	112·1 mph
1973	Silverstone	Peter Revson	McLaren-Ford	131·8 mph
1974	Brands Hatch	Jody Scheckter	Tyrrell-Ford	115·7 mph
1975	Silverstone	Emerson Fittipaldi	McLaren-Ford	120·0 mph
1976	Brands Hatch	Niki Lauda*	Ferrari	114·2 mph
1977	Silverstone	James Hunt	McLaren-Ford	130·4 mph
1978	Brands Hatch	Carlos Reutemann	Ferrari	116·6 mph

* Awarded first place after James Hunt's McLaren was disqualified

GERMAN GRAND PRIX

Year	*Circuit*	*Driver(s)*	*Car*	*Average speed*
1926	AVUS	Rudolf Caracciola	Mercedes	83·9 mph
1927	Nürburgring	Otto Merz	Mercedes-Benz	63·4 mph
1928	Nürburgring	Rudolf Caracciola and Christian Werner	Mercedes-Benz	64·6 mph
1929	Nürburgring	Louis Chiron	Bugatti	66·42 mph
1931	Nürburgring	Rudolf Caracciola	Mercedes-Benz	67·3 mph
1932	Nürburgring	Rudolf Caracciola	Alfa Romeo	74·24 mph
1934	Nürburgring	Hans Stuck	Auto Union	76·4 mph
1935	Nürburgring	Tazio Nuvolari	Alfa Romeo	75·2 mph
1936	Nürburgring	Bernd Rosemeyer	Auto Union	81·8 mph
1937	Nürburgring	Rudolf Caracciola	Mercedes-Benz	82·8 mph
1938	Nürburgring	Dick Seaman	Mercedes-Benz	80·7 mph
1939	Nürburgring	Rudolf Caracciola	Mercedes-Benz	75·3 mph
1950	Nürburgring	Alberto Ascari	Ferrari	77·7 mph
1951	Nürburgring	Alberto Ascari	Ferrari	83·7 mph
1952	Nürburgring	Alberto Ascari	Ferrari	82·1 mph
1953	Nürburgring	Giuseppe Farina	Ferrari	83·9 mph
1954	Nürburgring	Juan-Manuel Fangio	Mercedes-Benz	82·8 mph
1956	Nürburgring	Juan-Manuel Fangio	Ferrari	85·6 mph
1957	Nürburgring	Juan-Manuel Fangio	Maserati	88·8 mph
1958	Nürburgring	Tony Brooks	Vanwall	90·3 mph
1959	AVUS	Tony Brooks	Ferrari	143·6 mph
1960	*Nürburgring	Jo Bonnier	Porsche	80·3 mph
1961	Nürburgring	Stirling Moss	Lotus-Climax	92·3 mph
1962	Nürburgring	Graham Hill	BRM	80·3 mph
1963	Nürburgring	John Surtees	Ferrari	95·8 mph
1964	Nürburgring	John Surtees	Ferrari	96·6 mph
1965	Nürburgring	Jim Clark	Lotus-Climax	99·8 mph
1966	Nürburgring	Jack Brabham	Brabham-Repco	86·7 mph
1967	Nürburgring	Denny Hulme	Brabham-Repco	101·4 mph
1968	Nürburgring	Jackie Stewart	Matra-Ford	86·8 mph
1969	Nürburgring	Jacky Ickx	Brabham-Ford	108·4 mph
1970	Hockenheim	Jochen Rindt	Lotus-Ford	123·9 mph
1971	Nürburgring	Jackie Stewart	Tyrrell-Ford	114·4 mph
1972	Nürburgring	Jacky Ickx	Ferrari	116·6 mph
1973	Nürburgring	Jackie Stewart	Tyrrell-Ford	116·82 mph
1974	Nürburgring	Clay Regazzoni	Ferrari	117·3 mph
1975	Nürburgring	Carlos Reutemann	Brabham-Ford	117·7 mph
1976	Nürburgring	James Hunt	McLaren-Ford	117·2 mph
1977	Hockenheim	Niki Lauda	Ferrari	129·6 mph
1978	Hockenheim	Mario Andretti	Lotus-Ford	129·4 mph

* Formula 2 race, run on the Nurburgring South Circuit instead of the much longer North Circuit used normally.

ITALIAN GRAND PRIX

Year	Circuit	Driver(s)	Car	Average speed
1922	Monza	Pietro Bordino	Fiat	86·8 mph
1923	Monza	Carlo Salamano	Fiat	91·0 mph
1924	Monza	Antonio Ascari	Alfa Romeo	98·7 mph
1925	Monza	Gastone Brilli-Peri	Alfa Romeo	94·7 mph
1926	Monza	'Sabipa'	Bugatti	85·8 mph
1927	Monza	Robert Benoist	Delage	90·0 mph
1928	Monza	Louis Chiron	Bugatti	99·1 mph
1931	Monza	Giuseppe Campari and Tazio Nuvolari	Alfa Romeo	96·1 mph
1932	Monza	Tazio Nuvolari and Giuseppe Campari	Alfa Romeo	104·1 mph
1933	Monza	Luigi Fagioli	Alfa Romeo	108·5 mph
1934	Monza	Rudolf Caracciola and Luigi Fagioli	Mercedes-Benz	65·3 mph
1935	Monza	Hans Stuck	Auto Union	85·1 mph
1936	Monza	Bernd Rosemeyer	Auto Union	84·1 mph
1937	Livorno	Rudolf Caracciola	Mercedes-Benz	81·5 mph
1938	Monza	Tazio Nuvolari	Auto Union	96·7 mph
1947	Milan	Carlo Felice Trossi	Alfa Romeo	70·2 mph
1948	Turin	Jean-Pierre Wimille	Alfa Romeo	70·3 mph
1949	Monza	Alberto Ascari	Ferrari	105·0 mph
1950	Monza	Giuseppe Farina	Alfa Romeo	109·6 mph
1951	Monza	Alberto Ascari	Ferrari	115·9 mph
1952	Monza	Alberto Ascari	Ferrari	110·0 mph
1953	Monza	Juan-Manuel Fangio	Maserati	110·7 mph
1954	Monza	Juan-Manuel Fangio	Mercedes-Benz	111·9 mph
1955	Monza	Juan-Manuel Fangio	Mercedes-Benz	128·5 mph
1956	Monza	Stirling Moss	Maserati	129·7 mph
1957	Monza	Stirling Moss	Vanwall	120·3 mph
1958	Monza	Tony Brooks	Vanwall	121·2 mph
1959	Monza	Stirling Moss	Cooper-Climax	124·4 mph
1960	Monza	Phil Hill	Ferrari	132·1 mph
1961	Monza	Phil Hill	Ferrari	130·0 mph
1962	Monza	Graham Hill	BRM	123·6 mph
1963	Monza	Jim Clark	Lotus-Climax	127·7 mph
1964	Monza	John Surtees	Ferrari	127·8 mph
1965	Monza	Jackie Stewart	BRM	130·4 mph
1966	Monza	Ludovico Scarfiotti	Ferrari	135·9 mph
1967	Monza	John Surtees	Honda	140·5 mph
1968	Monza	Denny Hulme	McLaren-Ford	145·4 mph
1969	Monza	Jackie Stewart	Matra-Ford	146·9 mph
1970	Monza	Clay Regazzoni	Ferrari	147·0 mph
1971	Monza	Peter Gethin	BRM	150·7 mph
1972	Monza	Emerson Fittipaldi	Lotus-Ford	131·6 mph
1973	Monza	Ronnie Peterson	Lotus-Ford	132·63 mp
1974	Monza	Ronnie Peterson	Lotus-Ford	135·41 mp
1975	Monza	Clay Regazzoni	Ferrari	135·5 mph
1976	Monza	Ronnie Peterson	March-Ford	124·1 mph
1977	Monza	Mario Andretti	Lotus-Ford	128·0 mph

LE MANS 24-HOURS

Year	Drivers	Car	Average speed
1923	Lagache and Leonard	Chenard et Walcker	57·2 mph
1924	Duff and Clement	Bentley	53·7 mph
1925	De Courcelles and Rossignol	Lorraine	57·8 mph
1926	Bloch and Rossignol	Lorraine	66·0 mph
1927	Benjafield and Davis	Bentley	61·3 mph
1928	Barnato and Rubin	Bentley	69·1 mph
1929	Barnato and Birkin	Bentley	73·6 mph
1930	Barnato and Kidston	Bentley	75·8 mph
1931	Lord Howe and Birkin	Alfa Romeo	78·1 mph
1932	Sommer and Chinetti	Alfa Romeo	76·4 mph
1933	Sommer and Nuvolari	Alfa Romeo	81·4 mph
1934	Chinetti and Etancelin	Alfa Romeo	74·7 mph
1935	Hindmarsh and Fontes	Lagonda	77·8 mph
1937	Wimille and Benoist	Bugatti	85·1 mph
1938	Chaboud and Tremoulet	Delahaye	82·3 mph
1939	Wimille and Veyron	Bugatti	86·9 mph
1949	Chinetti and Lord Selsdon	Ferrari	82·3 mph
1950	Rosier and Rosier	Talbot	89·7 mph
1951	Walker and Whitehead	Jaguar	93·5 mph
1952	Lang and Riess	Mercedes-Benz	96·9 mph
1953	Rolt and Hamilton	Jaguar	105·9 mph
1954	Gonzalez and Trintignant	Ferrari	105·1 mph
1955	Hawthorn and Bueb	Jaguar	106·9 mph
1956	Flockhart and Sanderson	Jaguar	104·5 mph
1957	Flockhart and Bueb	Jaguar	113·9 mph
1958	P. Hill and Gendebien	Ferrari	106·1 mph
1959	Salvadori and Shelby	Aston Martin	112·6 mph
1960	Gendebien and Frere	Ferrari	109·2 mph
1961	Gendebien and P. Hill	Ferrari	115·9 mph
1962	Gendebien and P. Hill	Ferrari	115·2 mph
1963	Scarfiotti and Bandini	Ferrari	118·1 mph
1964	Guichet and Vaccarella	Ferrari	121·5 mph
1965	Rindt and Gregory	Ferrari	121·1 mph
1966	McLaren and Amon	Ford	125·4 mph
1967	Gurney and Foyt	Ford	135·4 mph
1968	Rodriguez and Bianchi	Ford	115·3 mph
1969	Ickx and Oliver	Ford	129·4 mph
1970	Attwood and Herrmann	Porsche	119·3 mph
1971	Van Lennep and Marko	Porsche	138·1 mph
1972	G. Hill and Pescarolo	Matra-Simca	121·5 mph
1973	Pescarolo and Larrousse	Matra-Simca	125·7 mph
1974	Pescarolo and Larrousse	Matra-Simca	119·3 mph
1975	Bell and Ickx	Gulf-Ford	118.9 mph
1976	Ickx and Van Lennep	Porsche	124·2 mph
1977	Barth, Heywood and Ickx	Porsche	121·0 mph
1978	Jaussaud and Pironi	Renault	130·5 mph

INDIANAPOLIS '500'

Year	*Driver*	*Car*	*Average speed*
1911	Ray Harroun	Marmon	74·6 mph
1912	Joe Dawson	National	78·7 mph
1913	Jules Goux	Peugeot	75·9 mph
1914	Rene Thomas	Delage	82·5 mph
1915	Ralph DePalma	Mercedes	89·8 mph
1916	Dario Resta	Peugeot	83·3 mph
1919	Howdy Wilcox	Peugeot	88·1 mph
1920	Gaston Chevrolet	Frontenac	88·2 mph
1921	Tommy Milton	Frontenac	89·6 mph
1922	Jimmy Murphy	Duesenberg	94·5 mph
1923	Tommy Milton	Miller	90·9 mph
1924	Lora Corum and Joe Boyer	Duesenberg	98·2 mph
1925	Pete DePaolo	Duesenberg	101·1 mph
1926	Frank Lockhart	Miller	95·9 mph
1927	George Souders	Duesenberg	97·5 mph
1928	Lou Meyer	Miller	99·5 mph
1929	Ray Keech	Miller	97·6 mph
1930	Billy Arnold	Miller-Hartz	100·4 mph
1931	Lou Schneider	Stevens-Miller	96·6 mph
1932	Fred Frame	Miller-Hartz	104·1 mph
1933	Lou Meyer	Miller	104·2 mph
1934	Bill Cummings	Miller	104·9 mph
1935	Kelley Petillo	Wetteroth-Offy	106·2 mph
1936	Lou Meyer	Stevens-Miller	109·1 mph
1937	Wilbur Shaw	Shaw-Offy	113·6 mph
1938	Floyd Roberts	Wetteroth-Miller	117·2 mph
1939	Wilbur Shaw	Maserati	115·0 mph
1940	Wilbur Shaw	Maserati	114·3 mph
1941	Floyd Davis and Mauri Rose	Wetteroth-Offy	115·1 mph
1946	George Robson	Adams-Sparks	114·8 mph
1947	Mauri Rose	Diedt-Offy	116·3 mph
1948	Mauri Rose	Diedt-Offy	119·8 mph
1949	Bill Holland	Deidt-Offy	121·3 mph
1950	Johnny Parsons	Kurits-Offy	124·0 mph
1951	Lee Wallard	Kurtis-Offy	126·2 mph
1952	Troy Ruttman	Kuzma-Offy	128·9 mph
1953	Bill Vukovich	KK500A-Offy	128·7 mph
1954	Bill Vukovich	KK500A-Offy	130·8 mph
1955	Bob Sweikert	KK500C-Offy	128·2 mph
1956	Pat Flaherty	Watson-Offy	128·5 mph
1957	Sam Hanks	Epperly-Offy	135·6 mph
1958	Jimmy Bryan	Epperly-Offy	133·8 mph
1959	Rodger Ward	Watson-Offy	135·9 mph
1960	Jim Rathmann	Watson-Offy	138·8 mph
1961	A. J. Foyt	Watson-Offy	139·1 mph
1962	Rodger Ward	Watson-Offy	140·3 mph
1963	Parnelli Jones	Watson-Offy	143·1 mph
1964	A. J. Foyt	Watson-Offy	147·4 mph
1965	Jim Clark	Lotus-Ford	150·7 mph
1966	Graham Hill	Lola-Ford	144·3 mph
1967	A. J. Foyt	Coyote-Ford	151·2 mph

Year	Driver	Car	Average speed
1968	Bobby Unser	Eagle-Offy*	152·9 mph
1969	Mario Andretti	Hawk-Ford*	156·9 mph
1970	Al Unser	PJ Colt-Ford*	155·7 mph
1971	Al Unser	PJ Colt-Ford*	157·7 mph
1972	Mark Donohue	McLaren-Offy*	162·9 mph
1973	Gordon Johncock	Eagle-Offy*	159·0 mph
1974	Johnny Rutherford	McLaren-Offy*	158·6 mph
1975	Bobby Unser	Eagle-Offy*	149·2 mph
1976	Johnny Rutherford	McLaren-Offy*	148·7 mph
1977	A. J. Foyt	Coyote-Foyt*	161·3 mph
1978	Al Unser	Lola-Cosworth*	161·4 mph

* Engines were turbocharged.

THE INDIANAPOLIS '500' IN PROFILE

Year	Formula and Reward
1911–12	Maximum capacity 600 cid (cubic inch displacement) relating to 9·83 litres *Purses from* $27,550–$55,225
1913–14	Maximum capacity 450 cid (7·37 litres) *Purses from* $55,875–$51,675
1915–16, 1919	Maximum capacity 300 cid (4·92 litres) *Purses from* $51,200–$55,275
1920–22	Maximum capacity 183 cid (2·99 litres) *Purses from* $93,550 *down to* $70,575
1923–5	Maximum capacity 122 cid (1·999 litres) *Purses from* $83,425–$87,750
1926–9	Maximum capacity 91·5 cid (1·499 litres) *Purses from* $88,100–$95,150
1930–37	Maximum capacity 366 cid (5·99 litres) *Purses from* $96,250–$92,135
1938–41, 1946–56	Maximum capacity 274·59 cid (4·49 litres) unsupercharged and 183·06 cid (2·999 litres) with supercharger. *Purses from* $91,075–$90,925 *and from* $115,450–$282,052
1957–66	Maximum capacity 256·284 cid (4·19 litres) unsupercharged and 170·856 cid (2·79 litres) supercharged *Purses from* $300,252–$691,808
1967	Maximum capacity for piston engines continued but turbines limited to 23-square inch inlet annulus area *Purse* $734,634, $171,227 *to the winner alone!*
1968	Piston engine limitations unchanged, turbine inlet annulus area slashed to 15·999 square inches *Purse* $712,269

In 1969 unsupercharged regulations continued as above, but 161·703 cid (2·65 litres) was set as the supercharged engine limit. Stock-blocks admitted up to 305·1 cid (4·999 litres) and turbines limited to 11·999 square inches, to be deleted in 1971. 1978 Rules were as on pp 174–5, as the reward approached **$1** million.

CONSTRUCTORS' INFORMAL CHAMPIONSHIP WINNERS 1950–57
WORLD FORMULA I CONSTRUCTORS' CHAMPIONSHIPS 1958–77

Year	*Constructor*	*Nationality*	*Year*	*Constructor*	*Nationality*
1950	Alfa Romeo	(I)	1964	Ferrari	(I)
1951	Alfa Romeo	(I)	1965	Lotus-Climax	(GB)
1952	Ferrari	(I)	1966	Brabham-Repco	(GB/AUS)
1953	Ferrari	(I)	1967	Brabham-Repco	(GB/AUS)
1954	Mercedes-Benz	(D)	1968	Lotus-Ford	(GB)
1955	Mercedes-Benz	(D)	1969	Matra-Ford	(F/GB)
1956	Ferrari	(I)	1970	Lotus-Ford	(GB)
1957	Maserati	(I)	1971	Tyrrell-Ford	(GB)
1958	Vanwall	(GB)	1972	Lotus-Ford	(GB)
1959	Cooper-Climax	(GB)	1973	Lotus-Ford	(GB)
1960	Cooper-Climax	(GB)	1974	McLaren-Ford	(GB)
1961	Ferrari	(I)	1975	Ferrari	(I)
1962	BRM	(GB)	1976	Ferrari	(I)
1963	Lotus-Climax	(GB)	1977	Ferrari	(I)

AMERICAN NATIONAL CHAMPIONS UNDER AAA SANCTION 1902–55

1902	Harry Harkness	1927	Pete DePaolo
1903	Barney Oldfield	1928	Lou Meyer
1904	George Heath	1929	Lou Meyer
1905	Victor Hemery	1930	Billy Arnold
1906	Joe Tracy	1931	Lou Schneider
1907	Eddie Bald	1932	Bob Carey
1908	Lewis Strang	1933	Lou Meyer
1909	George Robertson	1934	Bill Cummings
1910	Ray Harroun	1935	Kelly Petillo
1911	Ralph Mulford	1936	Mauri Rose
1912	Ralph DePalma	1937	Wilbur Shaw
1913	Earl Cooper	1938	Floyd Roberts
1914	Ralph DePalma	1939	Wilbur Shaw
1915	Earl Cooper	1940	Rex Mays
1916	Dario Resta	1941	Rex Mays
1917	Earl Cooper	1946	Ted Horn
1918	Ralph Mulford	1947	Ted Horn
1919	Howdy Wilcox	1948	Ted Horn
1920	Tommy Milton	1949	Johnnie Parsons
1921	Tommy Milton	1950	Henry Banks
1922	Jimmy Murphy	1951	Tony Bettenhausen
1923	Eddie Hearne	1952	Chuck Stevenson
1924	Jimmy Murphy	1953	Sam Hanks
1925	Pete DePaolo	1954	Jimmy Bryan
1926	Harry Hartz	1955	Bob Sweikert

Under USAC Sanction 1956–77

1956	Jimmy Bryan	1967	A. J. Foyt
1957	Jimmy Bryan	1968	Bobby Unser
1958	Tony Bettenhausen	1969	Mario Andretti
1959	Rodger Ward	1970	Al Unser
1960	A. J. Foyt	1971	Joe Leonard
1961	A. J. Foyt	1972	Joe Leonard
1962	Rodger Ward	1973	Roger McCluskey
1963	A. J. Foyt	1974	Bobby Unser
1964	A. J. Foyt	1975	A. J. Foyt
1965	Mario Andretti	1976	Gordon Johncock
1966	Mario Andretti	1977	Tom Sneva

Appendix 2

Organisations and Addresses

Motor Racing Publications

Autocar
Dorset House
Stamford Street
London SE1 9LU
England

Auto Motor und Sport
Postfach 1042
Leuchnerstrasse 1
7000 Stuttgart 1
West Germany

Autosport
76 Dean Street
London W1A 1BU
England

Auto Visie
Koningin Wilhelminalaan 12
Amersfoort
Holland

Bilen Motor og Sport
Palle Fogtal
Norre Farimagsgade 49
Copenhagen
Denmark

Bulletin Sportif de la FIA
8 Place de la Concorde
75008 Paris
France

Illustrerad Motor Sport
Tidningshuset
Fack 443 01
Lerum
Sweden

Motoring News
Standard House
Bonhill Street
London EC2A 4DA

National Speed Sport News
News Building (Box 608)
Ridgewood
New Jersey
USA

Rallye Racing
Frankfurterstrasse 22
Postfach 4869
62 Wiesbaden
West Germany

Automobile Revue
Nordring 4
3001 Bern
Switzerland

Autorevue
Graben 17
1010 Vienna
Austria

Auto Sport
1 Suwa-cho
Shinjuku-ku
Tokyo
Japan

Autoweek
13920 Mt McClellan Avenue
Reno
Nevada 89506
USA

Auto Zeitung
Graeffstrasse 5
5000 Cologne 30
West Germany

Car and Driver
One Park Avenue
New York
USA

Motor
Surrey House
Throwley Way
Sutton
Surrey

Motor Sport
Standard House
Bonhill Street
London EC2A 4DA

Racing Car News
PO Box 291
Broadway
NSW 2007
Australia

Road & Track
1499 Monrovia Avenue
Newport Beach
California 92663
USA

SA Motor
Scott House
41 Church Street
Cape Town
South Africa

Wheelspin News
3057 Universal Drive
Mississauga,
Ontario,
Canada

FORMULA 1 TEAMS

Arrows Racing Ltd
Milton Keynes
Buckinghamshire
England

Team Ensign,
Ensign Cars,
Queen's Drive
Queen's Street
Industrial Estate
Chasetown
Staffordshire
England

Copersucar-Fittipaldi
Fittipaldi Automotive Ltd
712 Banbury Avenue
Trading Estate
Slough
Buckinghamshire SL1 4LH
England

John Player Team Lotus
Wymondham
Norwich
Norfolk NR14 8EZ
England

Shadow Racing Team
Nichols Advanced Vehicles Systems Inc.,
Ross Road
Weedon Road Industrial Estate
Northampton
Northamptonshire
England

Tyrrell Racing Organisation Ltd
Long Reach
Ockham
Ripley
Surrey GU23 6PE
England

Sport Auto
41 Boulevard Barbes
70518 Paris
France

Brabham
Motor Racing Developments Ltd
Cox's Lane
Chessington
Surrey
England

Ferrari
Casella Postale 589
41100 Modena
Italia

Hesketh Racing
Easton Neston
Towcester
Northamptonshire
England

Renault
c/– 34 Quai du Pont du Jour
92109 Boulogne-Billancourt
Paris
France

Team Surtees Ltd
Station Road
Edenbridge
Kent TN8 6EH
England

Walter Wolf Racing Ltd
36 Bennett Road
Reading
Berkshire RG2 0QX
England

RACING DRIVER'S SCHOOLS

Great Britain
Brands Hatch Racing and Motor Racing Stables Ltd
Brands Hatch Circuit Ltd
Fawkham
Dartford
Kent DA3 8NG
England

Jim Russell School
Snetterton Circuit
Norwich
Norfolk NR16 2JX
England

Winfield Racing Drivers School
Goodwood
Chichester
West Sussex PO18 0PH
England

France
Ecole de Pilotage
AC de l'Ouest
Circuit des 24-Heures 19X
72040 Le Mans
France

Ecole de Pilotage Motul
BP 24
32110 Nogaro
France

Ecole de Pilotage Winfield
Circuit Paul Ricard
RN8
83330 Le Beausset
France

Ecole de Pilotage Winfield
Circuit de Magny-Cours
58470 Magny-Cours
France

Canada
Mosport Racing School
1905 Avenue Road
Toronto M5M 3Z9
Ontario
Canada

Jim Russell School
1065 Lakeshore Drive C-12
Dorval
Quebec H9S 3EI
Canada

Australia
Frank Gardner School
Corner Queensberry and Drummond Street
Carlton
Victoria 3053
Australia

Italy
Henry Morrogh School
Via Dante Alighieri 4
00063 Campagnano di Roma
Rome
Italy

USA
Skip Barber School
1000 Massachusetts Avenue
Boxboro
Massachusetts 01719
USA

Bob Bondurant School
Highways 37 & 121
Sonoma
California 95476
USA

Jim Russell School
PO Box 911
Rosamond
California 93560
USA

Further Reading

The field of motor racing books and periodicals is huge and varied both in scope and quality. The British weekly and monthly press as listed in the address session is generally of a very high standard, and very detailed, while the European magazines often have more in-depth personality reporting and quite outstanding photography. The American monthly *Road & Track* is noted for its Grand Prix race coverage, while the weekly *Autoweek* keeps well abreast of road and track-racing developments. *National Speed Sport News* is outstanding for its track race coverage at all levels.

Classics of motor racing literature still available (new and second hand) from specialised bookshops include biographical titles on Jack Brabham, Graham Hill, Jim Clark, Jochen Rindt, Bruce McLaren, Niki Lauda, James Hunt and many other great drivers such as Stirling Moss, Mike Hawthorn, and (if you can find them) Tazio Nuvolari, Hermann Lang and Rudi Caracciola. Marque histories have been produced in great detail on such subjects as Ferrari, Mercedes-Benz, Porsche, Lotus, Tyrrell, sections of the Maserati story, Jaguar, etc. There are also several motor racing encyclopaediae which are still available and more of which are published every year.

Specialised publications covering detail aspects of racing and regulations governing its various classes are available from the national sporting authorities in most countries, such as the Royal Automobile Club Motor Sports Division, 31 Belgrave Square, London SW1Y 5HW in Great Britain; The United States Auto Club, 4910 West 16th Street, Speedway, Indiana 46224, USA for their brand of track racing – NASCAR, PO Box K, Daytona Beach, Florida 32015, USA for stock car details – and the Sports Car Club of America, PO Box 22476, Denver, Colorado 80222, USA for road racing.

'How to do it' racing driver books appear from time to time.

One of the earliest works as an interesting period piece these days is Piero Taruffi's – the Italian works Ferrari, Maserati and Lancia (even Mercedes-Benz) driver – but Niki Lauda produced a more recent work called *Formula 1 – The Art and Technicalities of Grand Prix Driving* in its English-language edition, and Patrick Stephens Ltd of Cambridge, England, published the *Frank*

The name of the Game—Winning.

Gardner Castrol Racing Drivers Manual in 1973–4 which is more easily assimilated and which deals with less rarefied forms of racing as well as with Formula 1.

The same publisher is also responsible for the annual 'Yellow Book' – the *FIA Annuaire du Sport Automobile* or *FIA Year Book of Automobile Sport* and for the enthusiast who wants to appreciate deeply the regulations behind what is happening on an international level in his chosen sporting endeavour, this is recognised as being 'the bible'.

Illustration Credits

The author and publisher are most grateful to Geoffrey Goddard who provided most of the colour and black and white photographs for this book.

Full acknowledgments are as follows:

Geoffrey Goddard colour Plates 1–4, 6–32, 34–37, 40–43, 46, 48–61, 69–101 and photographs on pages 2, 11, 24, 26, 29, 33, 35, 38, 40, 43, 45, 48, 53, 58, 59, 60, 63, 64, 67, 73, 87, 89, 102 and 206.
Doug Nye colour Plates 63, 68, 103, 104, 105, 106 and photographs on pages 9, 15, 51, 82, 106 and 174.
Colorsport colour Plates 64, 65, 66 and 67.
Florida News Bureau photograph on page 172.
LAT colour Plates 33, 38, 39, 44, 45, 47, 62 and 102.
Cyril Posthumus photographs on pages x, 11, 22, 79 and 99.
Nigel Snowdon photograph on page 186.

The line illustrations of the racing circuits and the artwork for colour Plate 107 were prepared by David Dowland.

Index

Page numbers in *italics* refer to illustrations in the text. Figures in **bold** type are plate numbers in the colour section.